FMGE PRACTICE QUESTION BANK

NISHANT BHUSHAN

FOR MORE DETAILS PLEASE VISIT OUR WEBSITE
www.nishantbhushan.in

ABOUT THE AUTHOR

NISHANT BHUSHAN LIVES IN JAMSHEDPUR AND COMPLETED HIS 10TH FROM DAV BISTUPUR, FURTHER HE WENT TO SRI CHAITANIYA VIZAG FOR HIS HIGHER SECONDARY BOARDS AND FINALLY STARTED HIS JOURNEY BY PURSUING M.B.B.S FROM SRI LAKSHMI NARAYANA INSTITUTE OF MEDICAL SCIENCE PONDICHERRY.

PART-1

Q 1. All the following are derivatives of the neural crest, except:

A. Melanocyte

B. Adrenal medulla

C. Sympathetic ganglia

D. Cauda equina

Ans. D

Q 2. Which of the following is true regarding gastrulation:

A. Establishes all the three germ layers

B. Occurs at the caudal end of the embryo prior to

its cephalic end

C. Involves the hypoblastic cells of inner cell mass

D. Usually occurs at 4 weeks

Ans. A

Q 3. All the following features are seen in neurons from dorsal root ganglia, except:

A. They have centrally located nuclei

B. They are derived from neural crest cells

C. They are multipolar

D. They contain lipofuscin granules

Ans. C

Q 4. Elastic cartilage is found in:

A. Auditory tube

B. Nasal septum

C. Articular cartilage

D. Costal cartilage

Ans. A

Q 5. The weight of the upper limb is transmitted to the axial skeleton by:

A. Coracoclavicular ligament

B. Coracoacromial ligament

C. Costoclavicular ligament

D. Coracohumeral ligament

Ans. A

Q 6. The superficial external pudendal artery is a branch of:

A. Femoral artery

B. External iliac artery

C. Internal iliac artery

D. Aorta

Ans. A

Q 7. Diaphragmatic hernia can occur through all the following, except:

A. Esophageal opening

B. Costovertebral triangle

C. Costal and sternal attachment of diaphragm

D. Inferior vena cava opening

Ans. D

Q 8. Ureteric constriction is seen at all the following positions, except:

A. Ureteropelvic junction

B. Ureterovesicle junction

C. Crossing of iliac artery

D. Ischial spine

Ans. D

Q 9. All the following are true regarding blood supply to the kidney , except:

A. Stellate veins drain superficial zone

B. It is site of portosystemic anastomosis

C. The renal artery divides into five segmental arteries before entering the hilum

D. Its segmental arteries are end-arteries

Ans. B

Q 10. A patient with external hemorrhoids develops pain while passing stools. The nerve mediating this pain is:

A. Hypogastric nerve

B. Pudendal nerve

C. Splachnic visceral nerve

D. Sympathetic plexus

Ans. B

Q 11. Which of the following muscles is supplied by mandibular nerve:

A. Masseter

B. Buccinator

C. Tensor veli palati

D. Posterior belly of digastric

Ans. C

Q 12. The sensoy supply of the palate is through all of the following,

except:

A. Facial nerve

B. Hypoglossal nerve

C. Glossopharyngeal nerve

D. Maxillary division of trigeminal nerve

Ans. B

Q 13. All of the following are features of large intestine, except:

A. Large intestine secretes acidic mucus which helps in formation of stools

B. It is a site of mucocutaneous junction

C. Its epithelium contains globlets cells in large numbers

D. Absorbs salt and water

Ans. A

Q 14. In flexion and abduction of shoulder all of the following structures are compressed except:

A. Subacromial bursa

B. Long head of biceps

C. Suprascapular nerve

D. Supraspinatus tendon

Ans. C

Physiology

Q 15. SI unit for measuring blood pressure is:

A. Torr

B. mrnHg

C. kPa

D. Bar

Ans. C

Q 16. Glucose mediated insulin release is mediated through:

A. ATP dependent K+ channels

B. cAMP

C. Carrier modulators

D. Receptor phosphorylation

Ans. A

Q 17. Sudden decrease in serum calcium is associated with:

A. Increased thyroxine and PTH secretion

B. Increased phosphate

C. Increased excitability of muscle and nerve

D. Cardiac conduction abnormalities

Ans. C

Q 18. Ablation of the â€˜somatosensory area 1 of the cerebral cortex leads to:

A. Total loss of pain sensation

B. Total loss of touch sensation

C. Loss of tactile localization but not of two point discrimination

D. Loss of tactile localization and two point discrimination

Ans. D

Q 19. Non shivering thermogenesis in adults is due to:

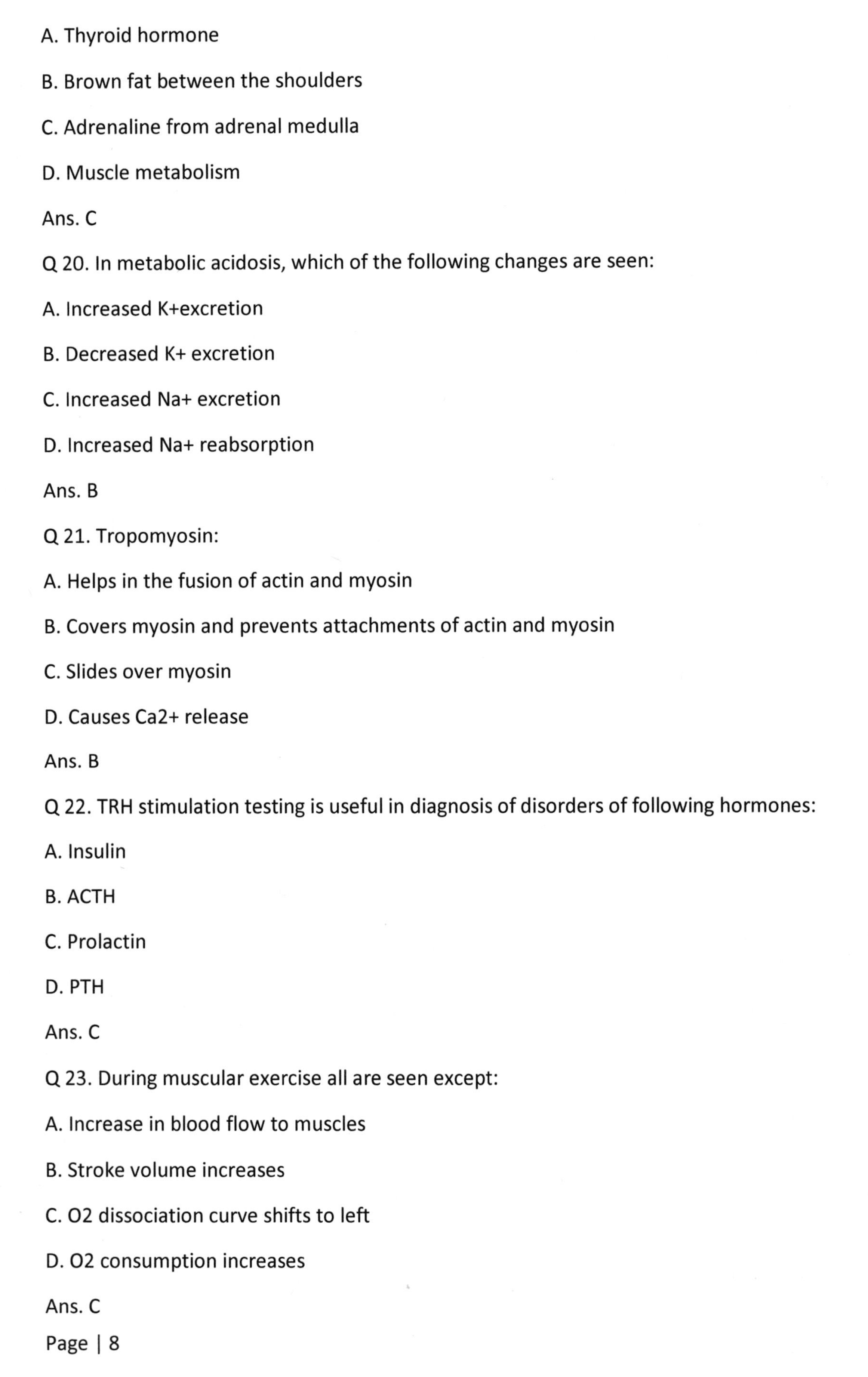

A. Thyroid hormone

B. Brown fat between the shoulders

C. Adrenaline from adrenal medulla

D. Muscle metabolism

Ans. C

Q 20. In metabolic acidosis, which of the following changes are seen:

A. Increased K+excretion

B. Decreased K+ excretion

C. Increased Na+ excretion

D. Increased Na+ reabsorption

Ans. B

Q 21. Tropomyosin:

A. Helps in the fusion of actin and myosin

B. Covers myosin and prevents attachments of actin and myosin

C. Slides over myosin

D. Causes Ca2+ release

Ans. B

Q 22. TRH stimulation testing is useful in diagnosis of disorders of following hormones:

A. Insulin

B. ACTH

C. Prolactin

D. PTH

Ans. C

Q 23. During muscular exercise all are seen except:

A. Increase in blood flow to muscles

B. Stroke volume increases

C. O2 dissociation curve shifts to left

D. O2 consumption increases

Ans. C

Q 24. â€œAll enzymes are not proteins.â€ This statement is justified by:

A. All enzymes do not follow the Michaelis Menten hypothesis

B. RNAs act as ribozymes

C. Antibodies take part in the catalysis of many reactions

D. Metals are involved in attachment to enzymes and catalysts

Ans. B

Q 25. Enzymes mediating transfer of one molecule to another are:

A. Transferases

B. Oxidases

C. Lysases

D. Peptidases

Ans. A

Q 26. In which of the following reactions is magnesium required:

A. Na+K+ ATPase

B. Dismutase

C. Phosphatase

D. Aldolase

Ans. A

Q 27. In oxidative phosphorylation, the ATP production and respiratory chain are linked by:

A. Chemical methods

B. Physical methods

C. Chemiosmotic methods

D. Conformational changes

Q Ans. C

Q 28. Thiamine level is best monitored by:

A. Transketolase level in RBC

B. Thiamine level in blood

C. G-6-PD activity

D. Reticulocytosis

Ans. A

Q 29. Vitamin B12 and folic acid supplementation in megaloblastic anemia leads to the improvement of anemia due to:

A. Increased DNA synthesis in bone marrow

B. Increased hemoglobin production

C. Erythroid hyperplasia

D. Increased iron absorption

Ans. A

Q 30. Nitric oxide synthase:

A. Is inhibited by Ca++

B. Catalyses a dioxygenase reaction

C. Accepts electrons from NADH

D. Requires NADH, FAD, FMN & heme iron

Ans. D

Q 31. Phenylalanine is the precursor of all the following, except:

A. Tyrosine

B. Epinephrine

C. Thyroxine

D. Melatonin

Ans. D

Q 32. In a well fed state, acetyl CoA obtained from diet is least used in the synthesis of:

A. Palmity CoA

B. Citrate

C. Acetoacetate

D. Oxalosuccinate

Ans. C

Q 33. Substrate level phosphorylation in citric acid cycle is seen in the conversion of: -ketoglutaratea

A. Acetoacetate to

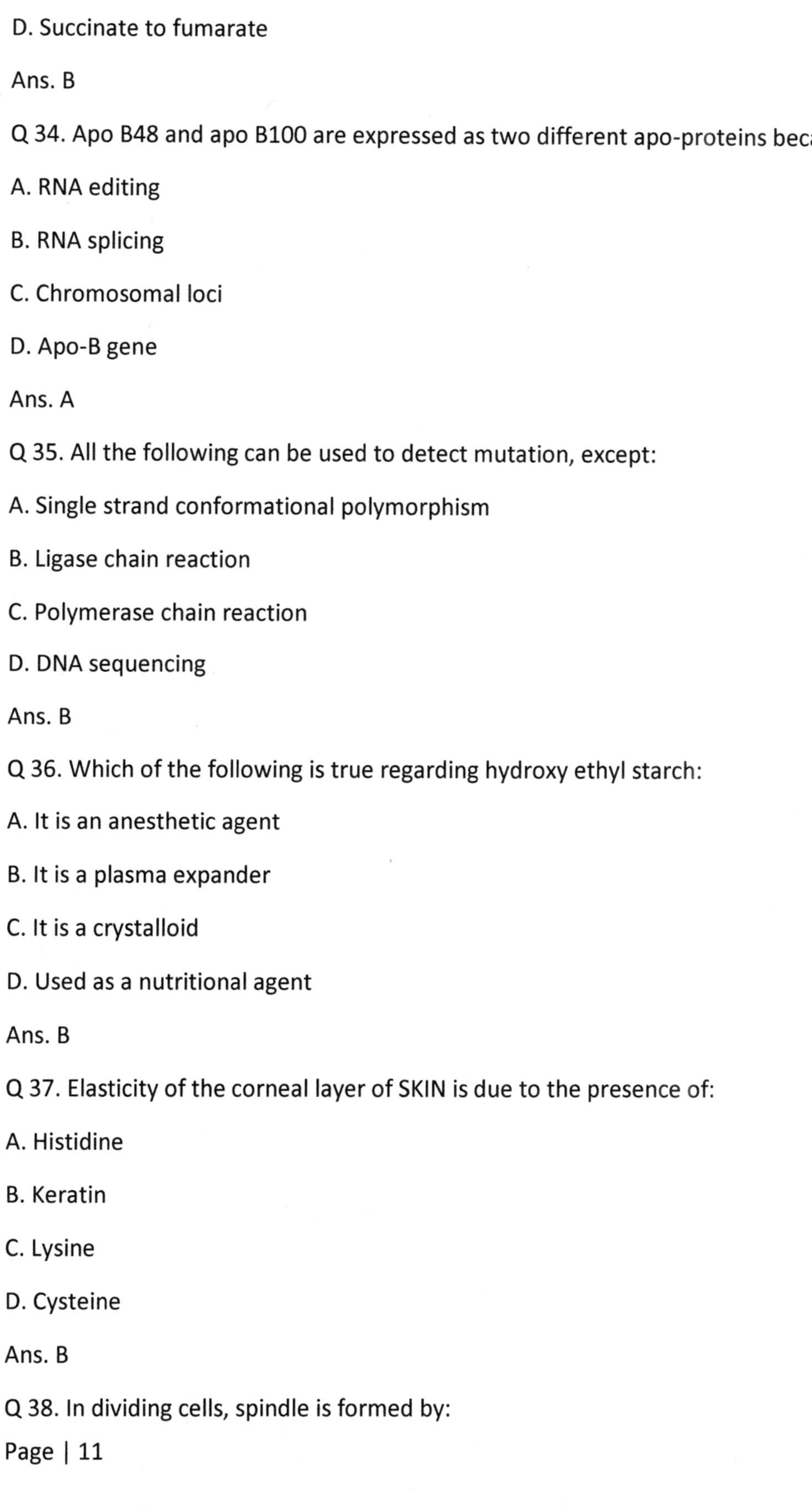

B. Succinyl CoA to succinate

C. Fumarate to malate

D. Succinate to fumarate

Ans. B

Q 34. Apo B48 and apo B100 are expressed as two different apo-proteins because of differe

A. RNA editing

B. RNA splicing

C. Chromosomal loci

D. Apo-B gene

Ans. A

Q 35. All the following can be used to detect mutation, except:

A. Single strand conformational polymorphism

B. Ligase chain reaction

C. Polymerase chain reaction

D. DNA sequencing

Ans. B

Q 36. Which of the following is true regarding hydroxy ethyl starch:

A. It is an anesthetic agent

B. It is a plasma expander

C. It is a crystalloid

D. Used as a nutritional agent

Ans. B

Q 37. Elasticity of the corneal layer of SKIN is due to the presence of:

A. Histidine

B. Keratin

C. Lysine

D. Cysteine

Ans. B

Q 38. In dividing cells, spindle is formed by:

A. Ubiquitin

B. Tubulin

C. Laminin

D. Keratin

Ans. B

Q 39. Entropy in a biological system is constant because:

A. It is an open system

B. It is a closed system

C. It is a governed by vitalism

D. Has exothermic-endothermic reactions

Ans. D

Q 40. Which of the following is true regarding a system which favours

oscillatory responses:

A. Has proportional component

B. Has a greater gain

C. Has a lesser gain

D. Positive FEEDBACK system

Ans. D

Q 41. Highest binding of iron is seen with:

A. Transferrin

B. Ferritin

C. Haemoglobin

D. Ceruloplasmin

Ans. C

Pathology

Q 42. The epitheloid cell and multinucleated gaint cells of granulomatous inflammation are derived from:

A. Basophils

B. Eosinophils

C. CD4 T lymphocytes

D. Monocytes-macrophages

Ans. D

Q 43. The following host tissue responses can be seen in acute infection, except:

A. Exudation

B. Vasodilation

C. Margination

D. Granuloma formation

Ans. D

Q 44. The following feature is common to both cytotoxic T cells and NK cells:

A. Synthesize antibody

B. Require antibodies to be present for action

C. Effective against virus infected cells

D. Recognize antigen in association with HLA class II markers

Ans. C

Q 45. In the intra-epithelial region of the mucosa of intestine the predominant cell population is that of:

A. B cell

B. T cells

C. Plasma cells

D. Basophils

Ans. B

Q 46. In primary tuberculosis, all of the following may be seen except:

A. Cavitation

B. Caseation

C. Calcification

D. Langerhan giant cell

Ans. A

Q 47. A mylocardial infarct showing early granulation tissue has most likely occurred:

A. Less than 1 hours

B. Within 24 hours

C. Within 1 week

D. Within 1 month

Ans. D

Q 48. A 10 year old boy, died of acute rheumatic fever. All the following can be expected at autopsy except:

A. Ashoff nodules

B. Rupture of chordae tendinae

C. McCallum patch

D. Fibrinous pericarditis

Ans. B

Q 49. All of the following are seen in asbestosis except:

A. Diffuse alveolar damage

B. Calcified pleural plaques

C. Diffuse pulmonary interstitial fibrosis

D. Mesotheliomas

Ans. A

Q 50. Macrophages containing large quantities of undigested and partial digested bacteria in intestine are seen in:

A. Whipples disease

B. Amyloidosis

C. Immunoproliferative small instetinal disease

D. Vibrio cholerae infection

Ans. A

Q 51. The histological features of celiac disease include all of the following, except:

A. Crypt hyperplasia

B. Increase in thickness of the mucosa

C. Increase in intraepithelial lymphocytes

D. Increase in inflammatory cells in lamina propria

Ans. B

Q 52. In a chronic alcoholic all the following may be seen in the liver except:

A. Fatty degeneration

B. Chronic hepatitis

C. Granuloma formation

D. Cholestatic hepatitis

Ans. C

Q 53. Crescent formation is characteristic of the following glomerular disease:

A. Minimal change disease

B. Rapidly progressive glomerulonephritis

C. Focal and segmental glomerulosclerosis

D. Rapidly non prgressive glomerulonephritis

Ans. B

Q 54. Necrotizing papillitis may be seen in all of the following conditions except:

A. Sickle cell disease

B. Tuberculous pyelonephritis

C. Diabetes mellitus

D. Analgesic nephropathy

Ans. B

Q 55. Disease or infarction of neurological tissue causes it to be replaced by:

A. Fluid

B. Neuroglia

C. Proliferation of adjacent nerve cells

D. Blood vessel

Ans. B

Q 56. Flat small vegetations in the cusps of both tricuspid and mitral valves are seen in:

A. Viral myocarditis

B. Libmann Sachs endocarditis

C. Rheumatic carditis

D. Infective endocarditis

Ans. B

Microbiology

Q 57. Bacteria may acquire characteristics by all of the following except:

A. Taking up soluble DNA fragments across their cell wall from other species

B. Incorporating part of host DNA

C. Through bacteriophages

D. Through conjugation

Ans. B

Q 58. Neonatal thymectomy leads to:

A. Decreased size of germinal center

B. Decreased size of paracortical areas

C. Increased antibody production by B cells

D. mcreased bone marrow production of lymphocytes

Ans. B

Q 59. Staphylococcus aureus differs from Staphylococcus epidermidis by:

A. Is coagulase positive

B. Forms white colonies

C. A common cause of UTI

D. Causes endocarditis in drug addicts

Ans. A

Q 60. Positive Shicks test indicates that person is:

A. Immune to diptheria

B. Hypersensitive to diptheria

C. Susceptible to diptheria

D. Carrier of diptheria

Ans. C

Q 61. In a patient with typhoid, diagnosis after 15 days of onset of fever is best done by:

A. Blood culture

B. Widal

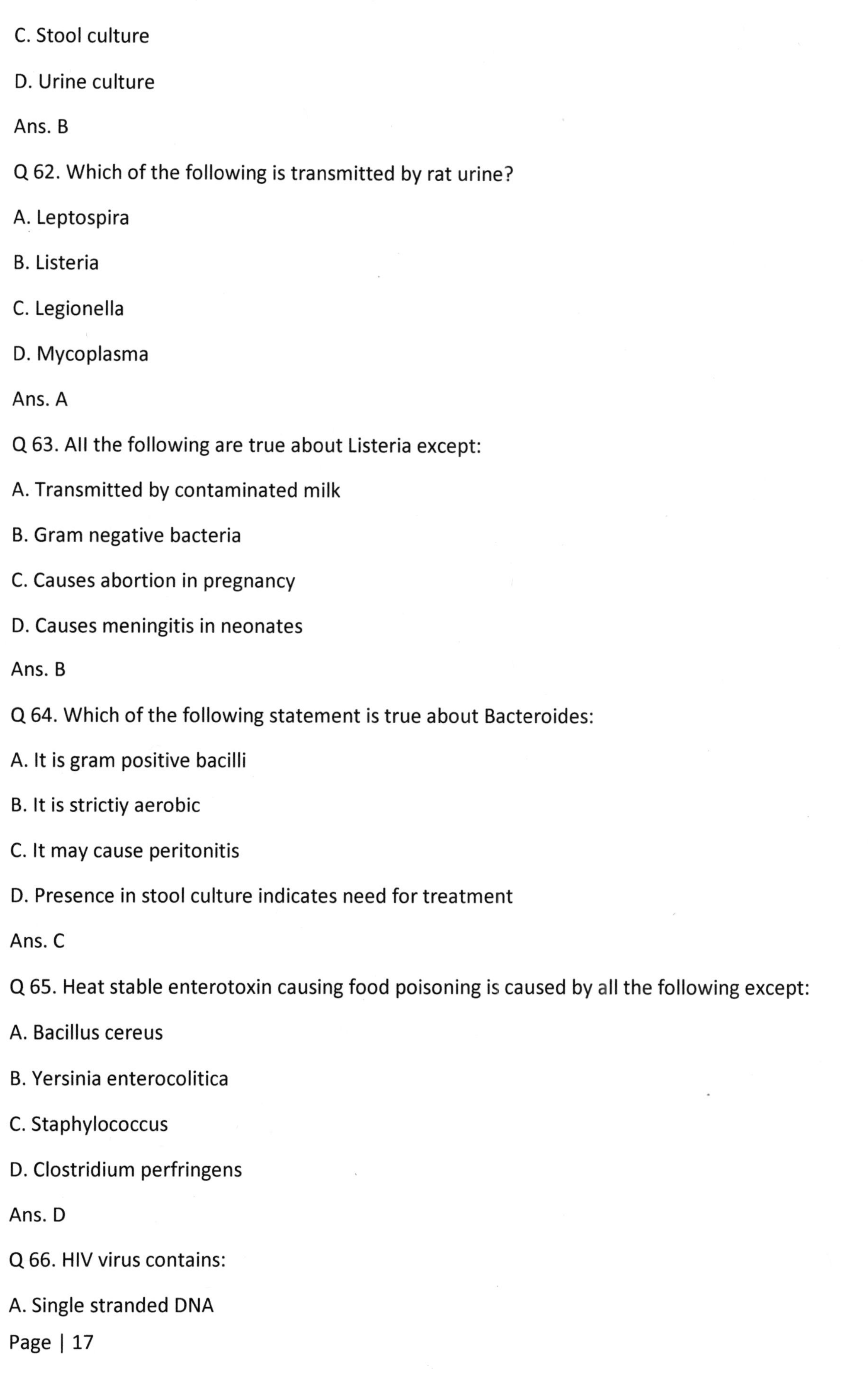

C. Stool culture

D. Urine culture

Ans. B

Q 62. Which of the following is transmitted by rat urine?

A. Leptospira

B. Listeria

C. Legionella

D. Mycoplasma

Ans. A

Q 63. All the following are true about Listeria except:

A. Transmitted by contaminated milk

B. Gram negative bacteria

C. Causes abortion in pregnancy

D. Causes meningitis in neonates

Ans. B

Q 64. Which of the following statement is true about Bacteroides:

A. It is gram positive bacilli

B. It is strictiy aerobic

C. It may cause peritonitis

D. Presence in stool culture indicates need for treatment

Ans. C

Q 65. Heat stable enterotoxin causing food poisoning is caused by all the following except:

A. Bacillus cereus

B. Yersinia enterocolitica

C. Staphylococcus

D. Clostridium perfringens

Ans. D

Q 66. HIV virus contains:

A. Single stranded DNA

B. Single stranded RNA

C. Double stranded DNA

D. Double stranded RNA

Ans. B

Q 67. Regarding HIV which of the following is not true:

A. It is a DNA retrovirus

B. Contains reverse transcriptase

C. May infect host CD4 cells other than T-lymphocytes

D. Causes a reduction in host CD4 cells at late stage of disease

Ans. A

Q 68. CMV retinitis in HIV occurs when the CD4 counts fall below:

A. 50

B. 100

C. 200

D. 150

Ans. A

Q 69. Epstein Barr virus causes all the following except:

A. Infectious mononucleosis

B. Measles

C. Nasopharyngeal carcinoma

D. Non Hodgkins lymphoma

Ans. B

Q 70. In a patient, corneal scraping reveals narrow angled septate hyphae. Which of the following is the likely etiologic agent:

A. Mucor

B. Aspergillus

C. Histoplasma

D. Candida

Ans. B

Q 71. Which of the following is true regarding globi in a patient with lepromatous leprosy:

A. Consists of lipid laden macrophages.

B. Consists of macrophages filled with AFB

C. Consists of neutrophils filled with bacteria

D. Consists of activated lymphocytes

Ans. B

Q 72. The following diagnostic tests are useful for corresponding purposes except:

A. Zeil-Neelson staining â€" Detection of mycobacteria

B. Immunoflorescence â€" Detection of influenza virus

C. Specific IgM antibodies â€" Immunity against rubella

D. Specific IgM antibodies â€" Detection of acute infection

Ans. C

Q 73. IL-1 produces:

A. T lymphocyte activation

B. Delayed wound healing

C. Increased pain perception

D. Decreased PMN release from bone marrow

Ans. A

Q 74. Microfilaria are seen in peripheral blood in which stage of filariasis:

A. Tropical eosinophilia

B. Early elephantiasis

C. Early adenolymphangitis stage

D. None of the above

Ans. C

Q 75. Confirmation of diagnosis of rota virus infection is by:

A. Antigen detection in stool by ELISA

B. Antibody titres in serum

C. Antigen detection by immunoflurescence

D. Antigen detection in serum by ELISA

Ans. A

Pharmacology

Q 76. Regarding efficacy and potency of a drug, all are true, except:

A. In a clinical setup, efficacy is more important than potency

B. In the log dose response curve, the height of the curve corresponds with efficacy

C. ED50 of the drug corresponds to efficacy

D. Drugs that produce a similar pharmacological effect can have different levels of efficacy

Ans. D

Q 77. All the following are selective beta blockers, except:

A. Atenolol

B. Esmolol

C. Bisprolol

D. Celiprolol

Ans. D

Q 78. All of the following factors increase the risk of aminoglycoside renal toxicity, except:

A. Elderly person

B. Dehydration

C. Simultaneous use with penicillin

D. Aminoglycoside administration in recent past

Ans. C

Q 79. In which of the following disorders is administration of barbiturates contraindicated in:

A. Anxiety disorders

B. Acute intermittent porphyria

C. Kemincterus

D. Refractive status epilepticus

Ans. B

Q 80. Mechanism of action tianeptin in the brain is:

A. Selective serotonin reuptake inhibition

B. Selective norepinephfine reuptake inhibition

C. Selective serotonin reuptake enchancer

D. Selective dopamine reuptake inhibition

Ans. C

Q 81. Proton pump inhibitors are most effective when they are given:

A. After meals

B. Shortly before meals

C. Along with H2 blockers

D. During prolonged fasting periods

Ans. B

Q 82. Which of the following is correctly matched:

A. Dimercaprol:Iron

B. Calcium di-sodium EDTA:Arsenic

C. Penicillamine:Copper

D. Desferrioxamine:Lead

Ans. C

Q 83. Digoxin is contraindicated in:

A. Supraventricular tachycardia

B. Atrial fibrillation

C. Congestive heart failure

D. Hypertrophic obstructive cardiomyopathy

Ans. D

Q 84. All the following drugs cause renal failure except:

A. Cephaloridine

B. Amphoterecin B

C. Cefoperazone

D. Gentamicin

Ans. C

Q 85. All of the following statements are true regarding losartan except:

A. It is a competitive angiotensin receptor antagonist

B. It has a long acting metabolite

C. Associated with negligible cough

D. Causes hyperuricemia

Q Ans. D

86. Gemcitabine is effective in:

A. Head and neck cancers

B. Pancreatic cancer

C. Small-cell lung cancer

D. Soft tissue sarcoma

Ans. B

Q 87. All of the following drugs can cross placenta except:

A. Phenytoin

B. Diazepam

C. Morphine

D. Heparin

Ans. D

Q 88. A highway truck driver has profuse rhinorrhea and sneezing. Which amongst the following durgs would you prescibe him?

A. Pheniramine

B. Promethazine

C. Dimerhydrinate

D. Cetrizine

Ans. D

Q 89. The mechanism of action of sodium nitroprusside is:

A. Increased cAMP

B. Increased guanylate cyclase

C. Calcium channel blockage

D. K+ channel opener

Ans. B

Q 90. All the following belong to the steroid receptor superfamily except:

A. Vitamin D3 receptor

B. Thyroid receptor

C. Retinoid receptor

D. Epinephrine receptor

Ans. D

Q 91. All of the following undergo hepatic metabolism before excretion except:

A. Phenytoin

B. Diazepam

C. Penicillin G

D. Cimetidine

Ans. C

Q 92. In a patient taking oral contraceptive, the chance of pregnancy increases after taking any of the following drugs except:

A. Phenytoin

B. Carbamazepine

C. Ampicillin

D. Cimetidine

Ans. D

Q 93. The primary mechanism of action of fluoride on topical application is:

A. Conversion of hydroxyapatite to fluoroapatite by replacing the â€“OH ions

B. Inhibition of plaque bacteria

C. Form a reservoir in saliva

D. Improvement in tooth morphology

Ans. A

Q 94. A 65 year old man was consuming opium for 20 years. He stops consumption suddenly and comes to casualty after 2 days. Which is likely to occur due to withdrawal:

A. Rhinorrhoea

B. Hypotension

C. Drowsiness

D. Miosis

Ans. A

Q 95. Which of the following causes hepatic granuloma?

A. Amiodarone

B. Alcohol

C. Cimetidine

D. Metronidazole

Ans. A

Q 96. Coronary steal commonly is seen with:

A. Atenolol

B. Diltiazem

C. Nitroglycerine

D. Dipyridamole

Ans. D

Q 97. A patient is taking ketoconazole for fungal infection develops cold for which he is prescribed terfenadine. Possible interaction between terfenadine and ketoconazole is:

A. Ketoconazole decreases metabolism of terfenadine

B. Terfenadine increases levels of ketoconazole

C. Ketoconazole decreases levels of terfenadine

D. No interaction

Ans. A

Forensic Medicine

Q 98. What would be the race of individual if skull bone having following feature â€" rounded nasal opening, horseshoe shaped palate, round orbit & cephalic index above 80:

A. Negro

B. Mongol

C. European

D. Aryans

Ans. B

Q 99. A sample to look for uric crystal (gouty tophus) would be submitted to the Pathology laboratory in:

A. Formalin

B. Distilled water

C. Alcohol

D. Normal saline

Ans. C

Q 100. Not a feature of brain death:

A. Complete apnea

B. Absent pupillary reflex

C. Absence of deep tendon reflex

D. heart rate unresponsive to atropine

Ans. C

Q 101. At autopsy, a body is found to have copious fine leathery froth in mouth & nostrils which increased on pressure over chest. Death was likely due to:

A. Epilepsy

B. Hanging

C. Drowning

D. Opium poisoning

Ans. C

Q 102. In fire arm injury, entery-wound blackening is due to:

A. Flame

B. Hot gases

C. Smoke

D. Deposition from bullet

Ans. D

Q 103. Tentative cut is a feature of:

A. Fall from the height

B. Homicidal assault

C. Accidental injury

D. Suicidal attempt

Ans. D

Q 104. Gastric lavage is indicated in all cases of acute poisoning ideally because of:

A. Fear of aspiration

B. Danger of cardiac arrest

C. Danger of respiratory arrest

D. Inadequat ventilation

Ans. A

Q 105. All of the following method used for detecting heavy metals, except:

A. Harrison & Gilroy test

B. Paraffin test

C. Neutron activation analysis

D. Atomic adsorption spectroscopy

Ans. B

Q 106. The sensation of creping, bugs over the body is a feature of poisoning due to:

A. Cocaine

B. Diazepam

C. Barbiturates

D. Brown sugar

Ans. A

Q 107. Which type of cattle poisoning occurs due to ingestion of linseed plant:

A. Aconite

B. Pilocarpine

C. Atropine

D. Hydro cyanic acid

Ans. D

Q 108. A 10 years old child present in casualty with snake bite since six hours. On examination no systemic signs are found & laboratory investigation are normal except localized swelling over the leg < 5 cm. Next step in management would be:

A. Incision & suction of local swelling

B. IV antivenom

C. Subcutaneous antivenom at local swelling

D. Observe the patient for progression of symptoms wait for antivenom therapy

Ans. D

Q 109. â€˜Gold chloride test is done in poisoning with:

A. Heroin

B. Barbiturates

C. Cocaine

D. Heavy metals

Ans. C

PREVENTIVE AND SOCIAL Medicine

Q 110. Iron and folic acid supplementation forms:

A. Health promotion

B. Specific protection

C. Primordial prevention

D. Primary prevention

Ans. B

Q 111. The most important function of sentinel surveillance is:

A. To find the total amount of disease in a population

B. To plan effective control measures

C. To determine the trend of disease in a population

D. To notify disease

Ans. A

Q 112. Serial interval is:

A. Time gap between primary and secondary case

B. Time gap between index and primary case

C. Time taken for a person from infection to develop maximum infectivity

D. The time taken from infection till a person infects another person

Ans. A

Q 113. All the following are advantages of case control studies except:

A. Useful in rare disease

B. Relative risk can be calculated

C. Odds ratio can be calculated

D. Cost effective and inexpensive

Q 114. The association between coronary artery disease and smoking was found to be as follows:

CAD No CAD

Smokers 30 20

Non smokers 20 30

The Odds ratio can be estimated as:

A. 0.65

B. 0.85

C. 1.35

D. 2.25

Ans. D

Q 115. In a prospective study comprising 10,000 subjects, 6000 subjects were put on beta carotene and 4000 were not, 3 out of the first 6000 developed lung cancer and 2 out of the second 4000 developed lung cancer. What is the interpretation of the above results?

A. Beta carotene is protective in lung cancer

B. Beta carotene and lung cancer have no relation to each other

C. The study design is not sufficient to draw any meaningful conclusions

D. Beta carotene is carcinogenic

Ans. B

Q 116. About direct standardization all are true except:

A. Age specific death rates are not needed

B. A standard population is needed

C. Population should be comparable

D. Two propulations are compared

Ans. A

Q 117. Which vaccine is contraindicated in pregnancy?

A. Rubella

B. Diphtheria

C. Tetanus

D. Hepatitis B

Ans. A

Q 118. Which of the following statements is true regarding pertussis?

A. Neurological complication rate of DPT is 1 in 50000

B. Vaccine efficacy is more than 95%

C. Erythromycin is useful for prophylaxis

D. The degree of polymorphonuclear leukocytosis correlates with the severity of cough

Ans. C

Q 119. Drugs A & B are both used for treating a particular SKIN infection. After one standard application, drug A eradicates the infection in 95% of both adults and children. drug B eradicates the infection in 47% of adults & 90% of children. There are otherwise no significant pharmacological differences between the two drugs, and there are no significant side effects. However, the cost of drug A is twice that of drug B. Dr. Sunil, a general practitioner, always uses drug B for the first treatment, and resorts to drug A if the infection persists. Dr. Sudhir, another general practitioner, always uses drug A for adults and drug B for children. Ignoring indirect costs, which of the following statement is incorrect:

A. Drug A is more effective than B for treating children

B. Drug A is more cost-effective than drug B for treating children

C. Drug A is more cost-effective than drug B for treating adults

D. Dr. Sudhirs regime achieves a higher level of cost-effectiveness than Dr. Sunils

Ans. B

Q 120. The infectivity of chicken pox lasts for:

A. Till the last scab falls off

B. 6 days after onset of rash

C. 3 days after onset of rash

D. Till the fever subsides

Ans. B

Q 121. Carriers are important in all the following except:

A. Polio

B. Typhoid

C. Measles

D. Diphtheria

Ans. C

Q 122. Acute flaccid paralysis is reported in a child aged:

A. 0-3 years

B. 0-5 years

C. 0-15 years

D. 0-25 years

Ans. C

Q 123. A 2-years-old boy, presented with cough, fever & difficulty in breathing. His RR 50/min. There was no chest indrawing. Auscultation of chest reveals bilateral crepitions. The most probable diagnosis is:

A. Very severe pneumonia

B. Severe pneumonia

C. Pneumonia

D. No pneumonia

Ans. C

Q 124. Active and passive immunity should be given together in all except:

A. Tetanus

B. Rabies

C. Measles

D. Hepatitis B

Ans. C

Q 125. Cereals and proteins are considered complemen-tary because:

A. Cereals are deficient in methionine

B. Cereals are deficient in methionine and pulse are deficient in lysine

C. Cereals are deficient in lysine and pulses are deficient in methionine

D. Cereal proteins contain non-essential amino-acids, while pulse proteins contain essential amino acids

Ans. C

Q 126. For a 60 kg Indian male, the minimum daily protein requirement has been calculated to be 40 g (mean) & standard deviation is 10. The recommended daily allowance of protein would be:

A. 60 g/day

B. 70 g/day

C. 40 g/day

D. 50 g/day

Ans. A

Q 127. A population study showed a mean glucose of 86 mg/ dL. In a sample of 100 showing normal curve distribution, what percentage of people have glocose above 86%?

A. 65 B. 50

C. 75 D. 60

Ans. B

Q 128. The best method to show the association between height and weight of children in a class is by:

A. Bar chart

B. Line diagram

C. Scatter diagram

D. Histogram

Ans. C

Q 129. The correlation between variables A and B in a study was found to be 1.1. This indicates:

A. Very strong correlation

B. Moderately strong correlation

C. Weak correlation

D. Computational mistake in calculating correlation

Ans. D

Q 130. The biological oxygen demand indicates:

A. Organic matter

B. Bacterial content

C. Anaerobic bacteria

D. Chemicals

Ans. A

Q 131. In a surveillance centre for hepatitis B, in a low prevalance area, the method for testing for hepatitis B was single ELISA. This policy was changed to double testing in series. This would result in the following 2 parameters of the test being affected:

A. Increased specificity and positive predictive value

B. Increased sensitivity and positive predictive value

C. Increased sensitivity and negative predictive value

D. Increased specificity and negative predictive value

Ans. A

Q 132. In a study, variation in cholesterol was seen before and after giving a drug. The test of significance would be:

A. Unpaired t test

B. Paired t test

C. Chi square test

D. Fisher test

Ans. B

Q 133. Ravi and Ashok stay in the same hostel of the same university. Ravi develops infection with group B meningococcus. After a few days Ashok develops infection due to group C meningococcus. All the following are true statements except:

A. Educate students about meningococcal trans-mission and take preventive measures

B. Chemotheraphylaxis to all against both group B and group C

C. Vaccine prophylaxis of contacts of Ravi

D. Vaccine prophylaxis of contacts of Ashok

Ans. C

Q 134. All of the following are common cause of post neonatal infant mortality in India, except:

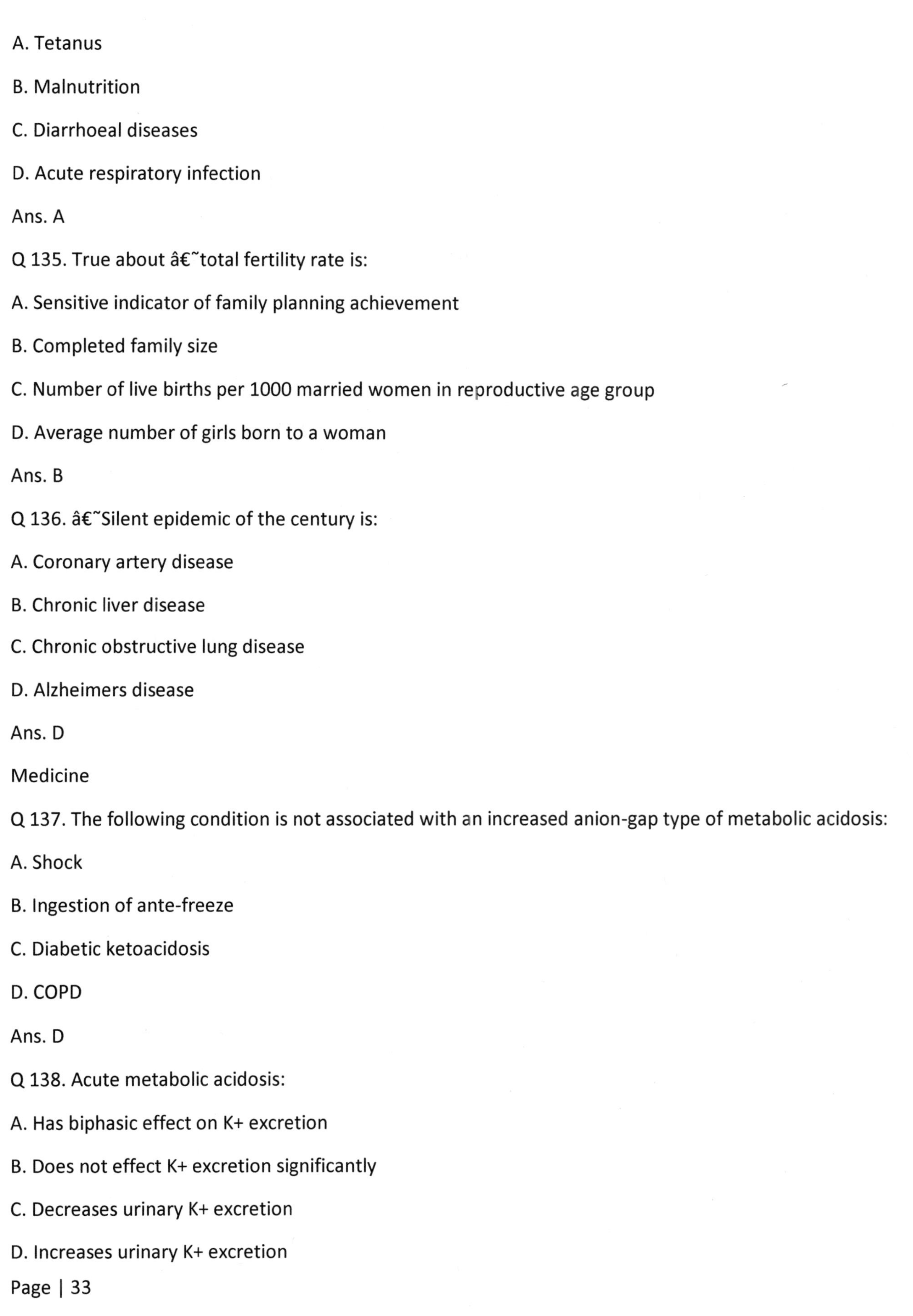

A. Tetanus

B. Malnutrition

C. Diarrhoeal diseases

D. Acute respiratory infection

Ans. A

Q 135. True about â€˜total fertility rate is:

A. Sensitive indicator of family planning achievement

B. Completed family size

C. Number of live births per 1000 married women in reproductive age group

D. Average number of girls born to a woman

Ans. B

Q 136. â€˜Silent epidemic of the century is:

A. Coronary artery disease

B. Chronic liver disease

C. Chronic obstructive lung disease

D. Alzheimers disease

Ans. D

Medicine

Q 137. The following condition is not associated with an increased anion-gap type of metabolic acidosis:

A. Shock

B. Ingestion of ante-freeze

C. Diabetic ketoacidosis

D. COPD

Ans. D

Q 138. Acute metabolic acidosis:

A. Has biphasic effect on K+ excretion

B. Does not effect K+ excretion significantly

C. Decreases urinary K+ excretion

D. Increases urinary K+ excretion

Ans. C

Q 139. Urinary anion gap an indication of excretion of:

A. Ketoacids

B. Na

C. H+ ion

D. K+ ion

Ans. B

Q 140. The most common mode of inheritance of congenital heart disease is:

A. Autosomal dominant

B. Autosomal recessive

C. SEX linked dominant

D. Multifactorial

Ans. D

Q 141. Which one of the following is an autosomal dominant disorder:

A. Cystic fibrosis

B. Hereditary spherocytosis

C. Sickle cell anemia

D. G-6-PD deficiency

Ans. B

Q 142. Which type diabetes is HLA associated:

A. Type I diabetes

B. Tyep II diabetes

C. Malnutrition related type disease

D. Pregnancy related type diabetes

Ans. A

Q 143. All of the following are sexually transmitted, except:

A. Candida albicans

B. Echionococcus

C. Molluscum contagiosum

D. Group B streptococcus

Ans. B

Q 144. All of the following infections may be transmitted via blood transfusion, except:

A. Parvo B19

B. Dengue virus

C. Cytomegalovirus

D. Hepatitis G virus

Ans. B Q 145. Hypoglycemia is a recognized feature of all of the following conditions except:

A. Uremia

B. Acromegaly

C. Addisons disease

D. Hepatocellular failure

Ans. B

Q 146. All of the following feature may be seen in thrombotic thrombocytopenic purpura, except:

A. Fever

B. HEMOLYSIS

C. Hypertension

D. Low platelet count

Ans. C

Q 147. The following laboratory determinants is abnormally prolonged in ITP:

A. APTT

B. Prothrombin time

C. Bleeding time

D. Clotting time

Ans. C

Q 148. PNH is associated with all of the following condition except:

A. Aplastic anemia

B. Increased LAP scores

C. Venous thrombosis

D. Iron deficiency anemia

Ans. B

Q 149. A 20 years adult presents with severe hypoplastic anemia. What is most effective treatment:

A. Interferona

B. IL-2

C. ATG therapy

D. Bone marrow transplant

Ans. D

Q 150. Which of the following is not commonly seen in polycythemia vera?

A. Thrombosis

B. Hyperuricemia

C. Prone for acute leukemia

D. Spontaneous severe infection

Ans. D

Q 151. The following condition is not associated with an anti-phopholipid syndrome:

A. Venous thrombosis

B. Recurrent foetal loss

C. Thrombocytosis

D. Neurological manifestations

Ans. C

Q 152. Hypergastrinemia with hypochlorhydria is seen in:

A. Zollinger-Ellison syndrome

B. VIPoma

C. Pernicious anemia

D. Glucagonoma

Ans. C

Q 153. All of the following phases of the jugular venous pulse and their causes are correctly matched, except:

A. â€˜cwave â€“ onset of atrial systole

B. â€˜a-x descent â€“ atrial relaxation

C. â€˜v-y descent â€“ emptying of blood from right atrium into right ventricle

D. â€˜y-a ascent â€“ filling of the right atrium from the vena cava

Ans. A

Q 154. Which of the following is the correct statement regarding findings in JVP:

A. Cannon wave: Complete heart block

B. Slow vy descent: Tricuspid regurgitation

C. Giant c wave: Tricuspid stenosis

D. Increased JVP with prominent pulsations:SVC obstruction

Ans. A

Q 155. While inseting a central venous catheter, a patient develops respiratory distress. The most likely cause is:

A. Hemothorax

B. Pneumothorax

C. Pleural effusion

D. Hypovolemia

Ans. B

Q 156. All of the following are clinical features of myxoma, except:

A. Fever

B. Clubbing

C. Hypertension

D. Embolic phenomenon

Ans. C

Q 157. Renal vein thrombosis is most commonly associated with:

A. Diabetic nephropathy

B. Membranous glomerulonephritis

C. Minimal change disease

D. Membranoproliferative glomerulonephritis

Ans. B

Q 158. Characteristic of Henoch-Schonlein purpura is:

A. Blood in stool

B. Thrombocytopenia

C. Intracranial hemorrhage

D. Susceptibility to infection

Ans. A

Q 159. Renal osteodystropy differs from nutritional and genetic forms of osesteomalacia in having:

A. Hypocalcaemia

B. Hypercalcemia

C. Hypophostaemia

D. Hyerphosphatema

Ans. D

Q 160. Medullary cystic disease of the kidney is best diagnosed by:

A. Ultrasound

B. Nuclear scan

C. Urography

D. Biopsy

Ans. D

Q 161. A patient with nephrotic syndrome on long-standing corticosteroid therapy may develop all the following except:

A. Hyperglycemia

B. Hypertophy of muscle

C. Neuropsychiatric symptoms

D. Suppression of the pituitary adrenal axis

Ans. B

Q 162. A 40 years old man presented with repeated episodes of bronchospasm and hemoptysis. Chest X-ray revealed perihilar bronchiectasis. The most likely diagnosis is:

A. Sarcoidosis

B. Idiopathic pulmonary fiborsis

C. Extrinsic allergic alveolitis

D. Bronchopulmonary aspergillosis

Ans. D

Q 163. Which of the following is characteristically not associated with the development of interstitial lung disease?

A. Coal dust

B. Sulfur dioxide

C. Thermophilic actenomycetes

D. Tobacco smoke

Ans. D

Q 164. A 35 years old man was found +ve for HBsAg and HBeAg, accidentally during screening of blood donation. On laboratory examination SGOT and SGPT are normal. What should you do next:

A. liver biopsy

B. Interferon therapy

C. Observation

D. HBV-DNA estimation

Ans. D

Q 165. A 25 years women presents with bloody diarrhea and is diagnosed as a case of ulcerative colitis. Which of the following condition is not associated:

A. Sclerosing cholengitis

B. Iritis

C. Ankylosing spondylitis

D. Pancreatitis

Ans. D

Q 166. Investigation of choice for invasive amebiasis is:

A. Indirect heamagglutination

B. ELISA

C. Counter immune electrophoresis

D. Microscopy

Ans. B

Q 167. A diabetic patient with BLOOD GLUCOSE of 600 mg/dL and Na 122 mEq/L was treated with insulin. After giving insulin the BLOOD GLUCOSE decreased to 100 mg/dL.What changes in blood Na level is expected?

A. Increase in Na+ level

B. Decrease in Na+ level

C. No change would be expected

D. Na+ would return to previous level spontaneously on correction of BLOOD GLUCOSE

Ans. A

Q 168. A 20 years young man presents with exertional dyspnoea, headache, and giddiness. On examination, there is hypertension and L VR. X-ray picture shows notching of the anterior ends of the ribs. The most like diagnosis is:

A. Pheochromocytoma

B. Carcinoid syndrome

C. Coarctation of the aorta

D. Superior mediastinal syndrome

Ans. C

Q 169. Rheumatoid factor in rheumatoid arthritis is important because:

A. RA factor is associated with bad prognosis

B. Absent RA factor rules out the diagnosis of rheumatoid arthritis

C. It is very common in childhood-rheumatoid arthritis

D. It correlates with disease activity

Ans. A

Q 170. Conns syndrome is associated with all except:

A. Hypertension

B. Hypernatremia

C. Hypokalemia

D. Oedema

Ans. D

Q 171. The triad originally described by Zollinger-Ellison syndrome is characterized by:

A. Peptic ulceration, gastric hypersecretion, non beta cell tumour

B. Peptic ulceration, gastric hypersecretion, beta cell tumour

C. Peptic ulceration, achlorhydria, non beta cell tumour

D. Peptic ulceration, achlorhydria, beta cell tumour

Ans. A

Q 172. All of the following are features of pheochromocytoma except:

A. Hypertensive paraoxysm

B. Headache

C. Orhtostatic hypotension

D. Wheezing

Ans. D

Q 173. The treatment of choice in young patient suffering from aplastic anaemia is:

A. Danazol

B. G-CSF

C. Bone marrow transplantation

D. ATG

Ans. C

Q 174. Raised anion gap in blood is not seen in which of the following?

A. Renal failure

B. Antifreeze ingestion

C. Diabetic ketoacidosis

D. Chronic respiratory failure

Ans. D

PEDIATRICS

Q 175. A Down syndrome girl has 21/21 translocation and her father is carrier of balanced translocation. Risk of Down syndrome in next pregnancy is:

A. 100%

B. 0%

C. 50%

D. 25%

Ans. A

Q 176. The following signs would warrant further evaluation of developmental status in a healthy 12 weeks old infant:

A. Dose not vocalize

B. Dose not babble

C. Dose not raise head up to 90Â°

D. Dose not transfer a bright red ring from one hand to the other, even when the ring is directly placed in the hand of child

Ans. A

Q 177. A 2 years child weighing 6.7 kg presents in the casualty with history of vomiting & diarrhoea for last 2 days. On examination SKIN pinch over the anterior abdominal wall go quickly to its original position. Interpretation of SKIN pinch test in this child will be:

A. No dehydration

B. Some dehydration

C. Severe dehydration

D. SKIN pinch can not be evaluated in this child

Ans. D

Q 178. An infant presents with history of seizures & SKIN rashes. Investigations show metabolic acidosis and increased blood ketone levels. This child is likely to be suffering from:

A. Propionic aciduria

B. Urea cycle disorder

C. Phenylketonuria

D. Multiple carboxylase deficiency

Ans. D

Q 179. With reference to RDS, all of the following statements are true, except:

A. Usually occurs in infants born before 34 weeks of gestation

B. Is more common in babies born to diabetic mothers

C. Leads to cyanosis

D. Is treated by administering 100% oxygen

Ans. D

Q 180. Which of the following is not a common manifestation of congenital rubella:

A. Deafness

B. PDA

C. Aortic stenosis

D. Mental retardation

Ans. C

Q 181. An 8 years old boy presented with fever and bilateral cervical lymphadenopathy with prior history of sore throat. There was no hepatomegaly. The peripheral blood smear shows > 20% lymphoplasmacytoid cells. The most likely diagnosis is:

A. Influenza

B. Tuberculosis

C. Infectious mononucleosis

D. Acute lymphoblastic leukemia

Ans. C

Q 182. The most common genetic cause of liver disease in children is:

A. Haemochromatosis

B. Antitrypsin deficiency1aB.

C. Cystic fibrosis

D. Glycogen storage disease

Ans. B

Q 183. Which of the following childhood tumors most frequently metastasizes to the bone:

A. Neuroblastoma

B. Ganglioneuroma

C. Wilms tumor

D. Ewings sarcoma

Ans. A

Q 184. A six months old girl is having recurrent UTI. Ultrasound abdomen shows bilateral hydronephrosis. MCU (micturating cystourethrogram) shows bilateral grade IV vesicoureteral reflux. The treatment of choice is:

A. Endoscopic injection of polyteflon at the ureteric orifices

B. Ureteric reimplantation

C. Bilateral ureterostomy

D. Prophylactic antibiotics

Ans. B

Q 185. The most common cause of ambiguous genitalia in a newborn is:

A. 21 hydroxylase deficiency

-hydroxylase deficiencybB. 11

C. -hydroxyalse deficiencya17

-hydroxysteroid deficiencybD. 3

Ans. A

Dermatology

Q 186. Multiple erythematous annular lesions with peripheral collarette of scales arranged predominantly over trunk are seen in:

A. Pityriasis versicolor

B. Pityriasis rubra

C. Pityriasis rosea

D. Pityriasis lichennoides

Ans. C

Q 187. All of the following are given for the treatment of pityriasis versicolor, except:

A. Ketoconazole

B. Griesofiilvin

C. Clotrimazole

D. Selenium sulphide

Ans. B

Q 188. A patient with PSORIASIS was started on systemic steroids. After stopping treatment, the patient developed generalized pustules all over the body. The cause is most likely to be:

A. Drug induced reaction

B. Pustular PSORIASIS

C. Bacterial infections

D. Septicemia

Ans. B

Q 189. Wickhams striae are seen in:

A. Lichen niditus

B. Lichenoid eruption

C. Lichen striates

D. Lichen planus

Ans. D

Q 190. Griseofulvin is given for the treatment of fungal infection in finger nail dermatophytosis for:

A. 4 weeks

B. 6 weeks

C. 2 months

D. 3 months

Ans. D

Q 191. After 3 days of fever patient developed maculoerythematous rash that lasted for 48 hours. The most likely diagnosis is:

A. Fifth disease

B. Rubella

C. Measles

D. Roseola infantum

Ans. D

Q 192. Exfoliative dermatitis can be due to all the following diseases, except:

A. Drug hypersensitivity

B. Pityriasis rubra

C. Pityriasis rosea

D. PSORIASIS

Ans. C

Q 193. Genital elephantiasis is caused by:

A. Donovanosis

B. Congenital syphilis

C. Herpes genitalis

D. Lymphogranuloma venereum

Ans. D

Psychiatry

Q 194. All of the following are features of hallucination, except:

A. Depends on will of the observer

B. Occurs in inner subjective space

C. It is a vivid sensory perception

D. It occurs in absence of perceptual stimulus

Ans. A

Q 195. The following is suggestive of an organic cause of the behavioural symptoms:

A. Formal thought disorder

B. Auditory hallucinations

C. Delusion of fruit

D. Visual hallucinations

Ans. D

Q 196. Delusion is not present in:

A. Delirium

B. Mania

C. Depresion

D. Compulsive disorder

Ans. D

Q 197. An alcoholic is brought to the casualty, 3 days after he quit alcohol, with the complaint of irrelevant talking. On examination, he is found to be disoriented in time, place and person. He also has visual illusions and hallucinations. There is no history of head injury. The most probable diagnosis is:

A. Dementia praecox

B. Delirium tremens

C. Schizophrenia

D. Korsakoff psychosis

Ans. B

Q 198. Ram Lal, a 45 years old male came to the psychiatric OPD complaning of continuous, dull, non-progressive headache for the last 8 years. The patient has seen numerous neurologists in the belief that he has a brain tumor even though all his investigations have been normal. The patient insisted that he had a brain tumor and requested yet another workup. Psychiatric evaluation reveals disease conviction in the background of normal investigations. The most probable diagnosis is:

A. Hypochondriasis

B. Somatization disorer

C. Somatoform pain disorder

D. Conversion disorder

Ans. A

Q 199. A patient presented with short lasting episodic behavioural changes which include agitation & dream like state with thrashing movements of his limbs. He does not recall these episodes & has no apparant precipitating factor. The most likely diagnosis is:

A. Schizophrenia

B. Temporal lobe epilepsy

C. Panic episodes

D. Dissociative disorder

Ans. D

Q 200. A young lady presented with repeated episodes of overeating followed by purging after use of laxatives. She is probably suffering from:

A. Bulimia nervosa

B. Schizophrenia

C. Aorexia nervosa

D. Binge eating disorder

Ans. A

Q 201. An 11 years old boy is all the time so restless that the rest of the class is unable to concentrate. He is hardly ever in his seat and roams around the hall. He has difficulty in playing quietly. The most likely diagnosis is:

A. Attention-deficit hyperactivity disorder

B. Conduct disorder

C. Depressive disorder

D. Schizophrenia

Ans. A

Surgery

Q 202. A patient suddenly experienced pain radiating along the medial border of the dorsum of foot. Which of the following nerve is most likely to be accidently ligated:

A. Sural nerve

B. Saphenous nerve

C. Deep peroneal nerve

D. Genicular nerve

Ans. B

Q 203. In an adult patient with pleural effusion, the most appropriate site for pleurocentesis done by inserting a needle is in:

A. 5th intercostal space in midclavicular line

B. 7th intercostal space in midaxillary line

C. 2nd intercostal space adjacent to the sternum

D. 10th intercostal space adjacent to the vertebral column

Ans. B

Q 204. Measurements of intravascular pressure by a pulmonary artery catheter should be done:

A. At end expiration

B. At peak of inspiration

C. During mid inspiration

D. During mid expiration

Ans. A

Q 205. A 24 years old man falls on the ground when he is struck in the right temple by a baseball. While being driven to the hospital, he lapses into coma. He is unresponsive with the dilated right pupil when he reaches the emergency department. The most important step in initial management is:

A. Craniotomy

B. CT scan of the head

C. X-ray of the skull and cervical spine

D. Doppler ultrasound examination of the neck

Ans. A

Q 206. Kamla Rani, 75 years old woman, presents after 6 weeks with post myocardial infarction with mild CHF. There was past history of neck Surgery for parathyroid adenoma 5 years ago. EKG shows slow artrial fibrillation. Serum Ca2+ 13.0 mg/L and urinary Ca2+ is 300 g/24 h. On examination these is small mass in the paratracheal position behind the right clavicle. Appropriate management at this time is:

A. Repeat neck Surgery

B. Treatment with technetium -99

C. Observation and repeat serum Ca2+ in two months

D. Ultrasound-guided alcohol injection of the mass

Ans. D

Q 207. Not a feature of de Quervains disease:

A. Autoimmune in etiology

B. Raised ESR

C. Tends to regress spontaneously

D. Painful & associated with enlargement of thyroid

Ans. A

Q 208. A 35 years old woman has had recurrent episodes of headache and sweating. Her mother had renal calculi and died of thyroid cancer. Physical observations revealed a thyroid nodule and ipsilateral enlarged cervical lymph nodes. Before performing thyroid Surgery the womans physician should order:

A. Thyroid scan

B. Estimation of hydroxy indole acetic acid in urine

C. Estimation of urinary metanephrines, VMA and catecholamines

D. Estimation of TSH, and TRH levels in serum

Ans. C

Q 209. All of the following are associated with thyroid storm, except:

A. Surgery for thyroiditis

B. Surgery for thyrotoxicosis

C. Stressful illness in thyrotoxicosis

D. I131 therapy for thyrotoxicosis

Ans. A

Q 210. Needle biopsy of solitary thyroid nodule in a young woman with palpable cervical lymph nodes on the same sides demonstrates amyloid in stroma of lesion. Likely diagnosis is:

A. Medullary carcinoma thyroid

B. Follicular carcinoma thyroid

C. Thyroid adenoma

D. Multinodular goitre

Ans. A

Q 211. A 26 years old woman presents with a palpable thyroid nodule, and needle biopsy demonstrates amyloid in the stroma of the lesion. A cervical lymph node is palpable on the same side as the lesion. The preferred treatment should be:

A. Removal of the involved node, the isthmus,and the enlarged lymph node

B. Removal of the involved lobe, the isthmus, a portion of the opposite lobe, and the enlarged lymph node

C. Total thyroidectomy and modified neck dissection on the side of the enlarged lymph node

D. Total thyroidectomy and irradiation of the cervical lymph nodes

Ans. C

Q 212. The most common tumor of the salivary gland is:

A. Mucoepidermoid tumor

B. Warthins tumor

C. Acinic cell tumor

D. Pleomorphic adenoma

Ans. D

Q 213. The premalignant condition with the highest probability of progression to malignancy is:

A. Dysplasia

B. Hyperplasia

C. Leucoplakia

D. Erythroplakia

Ans. D

Q 214. An old man who is edentulous developed squamous cell CA in buccal mucosa that has infiltrated to the alveolus. Following is not indicated in treatment:

A. Radiotherapy

B. Segmental mandibulectomy

C. Marginal mandibulectomy involving removal of the outer table only

D. Marginal mandibulectomy involving removal of upper half of mandible

Ans. C

Q 215. Corkscrew esophagus is seen in which of the following condition?

A. Carcinoma esophagus

B. Scleroderma

C. Achalasia cardia

D. Diffuse esophagus spasm

Ans. D

Q 216. Treatment for achalasia associated with high rate of recurrence:

A. Pneumatic dilatation

B. Laparoscopic myotomy

C. Opefl surgical myotomy

D. Botulinum toxin

Ans. D

Q 217. Barretts esophagus is:

A. Lower esophagus lined by columnar epithelium

B. Upper esophagus lined by columnar epithelium

C. Lower esophagus lined by ciliated epithelium

D. Lower esophagus lined by pseudostratified epithelium

Ans. A

Q 218. The adenocarcinoma of esophagus developes in:

A. Barretts esophagus

B. Long standing achalasia

C. Corrosive stricture

D. Alcohol abuse

Ans. A

Q 219. The lowest recurrence of peptic ulcer is associated with:

A. Gastric resection

B. Vagotomy + drainage

C. Vagotomy + antrectomy

D. Highly selective vagotomy

Ans. C

Q 220. Risk factor for development of gastric CA:

A. Blood group O

B. Duodenal ulcer

C. Intestinal hyperplasia

D. Intestinal metaplasia type III

Ans. D

Q 221. In a case of hypertrophic pyloric stenosis, the metabolic disturbance is:

A. Respiratory alkalosis

B. Metabolic acidosis

C. Metabolic alkalosis with paradoxical aciduria

D. Metabolic alkalosis with alkaline urine

Ans. C

Q 222. All the following indicates early gastric cancer except:

A. Involvement of mucosa

B. Involvement of mucosa and submucosa

C. Involvement of mucosa, submucosa and muscularis

D. Involvement of mucosa, submucosa and adjacent lymph nodes

Ans. C

Q 223. In gastric outlet obstruction in a peptic ulcer patient, the site of obstruction is most likely to be:

A. Antrum

B. Duodenum

C. Pylorus

D. Pyloric canal

Ans. B

Q 224. Ramesh met an accident with a car and has been in â€˜deep coma for the last 15 days. The most suitable route for the administration of protein and calories is by:

A. Jejunostomy tube feeding

B. Gastrostomy tube feeding

C. Nasogastric tube feeding

D. Central venous hyperalimentation

Ans. A

Q 225. A 10 months old infant present with acute intestinal obstruction. Contrast enema X-ray shows the intussusception. Likely cause is:

A. Peyers patch hypertrophy

B. Mekels diverticulum

C. Mucosal polyp

D. Duplication cyst

Ans. A

Q 226. After undergoing Surgery , for carcinoma of colon, a 44 year old patient developed single liver metastasis of 2 cm. What do you do next:

A. Resection

B. Chemo-radiation

C. Acetic acid injection

D. Radiofrequency ablation

Ans. A

Q 227. Ten days after a splenectomy for blunt abdominal trauma, a 23 years old man complains of upper abdominal and lower chest pain exacerbated by deep breathing. He is anorectic but ambulatory and otherwise making satisfactory progress. On physical examination, his temperature is 38.2Â°C (108Â°F) rectally, and he has decreased breath sounds at the left lung base. His abdominal wound appears to be healing well. bowel sound are active and there are no peritoneal signs. Rectal examination is negative. The WBC count is 12,500 per mm3 with a shift to left. Chest X-ray shows plate like atelectasis of the left lung field. Abdominal X-rays show a nonspecific gas pattern in the bowel and an air-fluid level in the left upper quadrant. Serum amylase is 150 Somogyi units/ dl (normal 60 to 80). The most likely diagnosis is:

A. Subphrenic abscess

B. Pancreatitis

C. Pulmonary embolism

D. Subfascial wound infection

Ans. A

Q 228. Sentinel lymph node biopsy is an important part of the management of which of the following conditions?

A. Carcinoma prostate

B. Carcinoma breast

C. Carcinoma lung

D. Carcinoma nasopharynx

Ans. B

Q 229. A man who weighs 70 kg (154 pounds) is transfered to a burn center 4 weeks after sustaining a second and third-degree burn injury to 45% of his total body surface area. Prior to accident, the patients weight was 90 kg (198 pounds). The patient has not been given anything by mouth since the injury except for antacids because of previous ulcer history. On physical examination, the patients burn wounds are clean, but only minimal healing is evident and thick adherent eschar is present. The patients abdomen is soft and nondistended, and active bowel sounds are heard. His stools are trace-positive for blood, and he has a right inguinal hernia, which appears to be easily reducible. He has poor range of motion of all involved joints and has developed early axillary and popliteal fossae flexion contractures. In managing this patient at this stage of his injury, top priority must be given to correcting:

A. The presence of blood in stools by the increasing the dose of antacids and H1 receptor blocker

B. The open, poorly healing burn wounds treated by surgical excision and grafting

C. The inguinal hernia treated by surgical repair using local Anaesthesia

D. The nutritional status by oral supplementation or parenteral hyperalimentation

Ans. D

Q 230. A 14 years old girl sustains a steam bum measuring 6 by 7 inches over the ulnar aspect of her right forearm. Blisters develop over the entire area of the bum wound, and by the time the patient is seen 6 hours after the injury, some of the blisters have ruptured spontaneously. In addition to debridement of the necrotic epithelium, all the following

therapeutic regiments might be considered appropriate for this patient except:

A. Application of silver sulfadiazine and daily washes, but no dressing

B. Application of polyvinylpyrrolidone foam, daily washes and a light occlusive dressing changed daily

C. Application of mafenide acetate cream, but no daily washes or dressing

D. Heterograft application with sutures to secure it in place and daily washes, but no dressing

Ans. D

Q 231. All of the following are the clinical features of thromboangitis obliterans except:

A. Raynauds phenomenon

B. Claudication of extremeties

C. Absence of popliteal pulse

D. Migratory superficial thrombophlebitis

Ans. C

Q 232. Rani, a 16 years old girl who has non-pitting edema of recent onset affecting her right leg but no other symptoms is referred for evaluation. True statements about this patient include:

A. Prophylactic antibiotics are indicated

B. A lymphagiongram will show hypoplasia of the lymphatics

C. Elastic stocking and diuretics will lead to a normal appearance of the limb

D. A variety of operations will ultimately lead to a normal appearance of the limb

Ans. B

Q 233. Kamla, a 59 years old woman, has a left femoral vein thrombosis during a pregnancy 30 year ago. The left greater saphenous vein had been stripped at age 21. She now presents with a large non healing ulceration over the medial left calf, which has continuously progressed despite bedrest, elevation, and use of a support stocking. Descending phlebography of the left leg demonstrates a patent deep venous system, with free flow of dye from the groin to foot. The first profunda femoris valve is competent. Appropriate management might include which of the following:

A. Division of the superficial femoral vein in the groin and transposition of its distal end onto the profunda femoris vein below the level of the competent profunda valve

B. Saphenous venous crossover graft with anastomosis of the end of the right saphenous vein onto the side of competent femoral vein

C. Ligated iliofemoral venous thrombectomy with creation of the temporary arteriovenous fistula

D. Subfascial ligation of perforating veins in the left calf.

Ans. A

Q 234. On her third day of hospitalization, a 70 years old woman who is being treated with antibiotics for acute cholecystitis develops increased pain and tenderness in the right upper quadrant with a palpable mass. Her temperature rises to 40Â°C (104Â°F) her blood pressure falls to 80/60 mmHg. Hematemesis, and melena ensue and petechiae are noted. Laboratory studies reveal thrombocytopenia, prolonged prothrombin time, and a decreased fibrinogen level. The most important step in the correction of this patients coagulopathy is:

A. Exploratory laparotomy

B. Administration of heparin

C. Administration of aminocaproic acide

D. Administration of fresh frozen plasma

Ans. A

Q 235. A 64 years old previously healthy man is admitted to a hospital because of a closed head injury and ruptured spleen following a road side automobile accident. During the first 4 days of hospitalization, following laparotomy and splenectomy, he receives 5% dextrose, 0.5% normal saline solution at a rate of 125 mL/h. Recorded daily fluid outputs include 450 to 600 mL of nasogastric drainage and 700 to 1000 mL of urine. The patient

is somnolent but easily aroused until the morning of the 5th hospital day, when he is noted to be in deep coma. By the afternoon, he begins having seizures. The following laboratory data are obtained. Serum electrolytes (mEq/L): Na+ 130; K+ 1.9; Clâ€“ 96; HCO3â€“ 19. Serum osmolality 260 mOsm/L. Urine electrolytes (mEq/L): Na+ 61; K+ 18. Which of the following statements about diagnosis or treatment of this patients condition is true:

A. Emergency carotid arteriogram is to be done

B. Secondary to metabolic acidosis there is hypokalemia

C. A small qantity of hypertonic saline should be given

D. IV infusion of 20 ml of 50% MgSO4 is given over a period of 4 hours

Ans. C

Q 236. All of the following statements about acute adrenal insufficiency are true except:

A. Hyperglycemia is usually present

B. Acute adrenal insufficiency usually is secondary to exogenous glucocorticoid administration

C. Acute adrenal insufficiency presents with weakness, vomiting, fever, and hypotension

D. Hyponatremia occurs because of impaired renal tubule sodium resorption

Ans. A

Q 237. All of the following are correct statements about radiological evaluation of a pateint with Cushings syndrome except:

A. MRI of the sella turcica will identify a pituitary cause for Cushings syndrome

B. Petrosal sinus sampling is the best way to distinguish a pituitary tumor from an ectopic ACTH producing tumor.

C. MRI of the adrenals may distinguish adrenal adenoma from carcinoma

D. Adrenal CT scan distinguishes adrenal cortical hyperplasia from an adrenal tumor

Ans. A

Orthopaedics

Q 238. Carpel tunnel syndrome is due to compression of:

A. Radial nerve

B. Ulnar nerve

C. Palmar branch of the ulnar nerve

D. Median nerve

Ans. D

Q 239. Most common nerve involved in the FRACTURE of surgical neck of humerus is:

A. Median

B. Radial

C. Ulnar

D. Axillary

Ans. D

Q 240. All of the following are associated with supracondylar FRACTURE of humerus, except:

A. It is uncommon after 15 years of age

B. Extension type FRACTURE is more common than the flexion type

C. Cubitus varus deformity commonly results following malunion

D. Ulnar nerve is most commonly involved

Ans. D

Q 241. A 40 years old man, was admitted with FRACTURE shaft femur following a road traffic accident. On 2nd day he became disoriented. He was found to be tachypnoeic, and had conjunctival petechiae. Most likely diagnosis is:

A. Pulmonary embolism

B. Sepsis syndrome

C. Fat embolism

D. Haemothorax

Ans. C

Q 242. Kumar, a 31 years old motorcyclist sustained injury over his right hip joint. X-ray revealed a posterior dislocation of the right hip joint. The clinical attitude of the affected lower limb will be:

A. External rotation, extension & abduction

B. Internal rotation, flexion & adduction

C. Internal rotation, extension & abduction

D. External rotation, flexion & abduction

Ans. B

Q 243. Pappu, 7 years old young boy, had FRACTURE of lateral condyle of femur. He developed malunion as the FRACTURE was not reduced anatomically. Malunion will produce:

A. Genu valgum

B. Genu varum

C. Genu recurvatum

D. Dislocation of knee

Ans. A

Q 244. Patellar tendon bearing POP cast is indicated in the following FRACTURE :

A. Patella

B. Tibia

C. Medial malleolus

D. Femur

Ans. B

Q 245. Inversion injury at the ankle can cause all of the following except:

A. FRACTURE tip of lateral melleolus

B. FRACTURE base of the 5th metatarsal

C. Sprain of extensor digitorum brevis

D. FRACTURE of sustentaculam tali

Ans. C

Q 246. A previously healthy 45 years old laborer suddenly develops acute lower back pain with right-leg pain & weakness of dorsiflexion of the right great toe. Which of the following is true:

A. Immediate treatment should include analgesics, muscle relaxants & back strengthening exercises

B. The appearance of the foot drop indicates early surgical intervention

C. If the neurological signs resolve within 2 to 3 weeks but low back pain persists, the proper treatment would include fusion of affected lumbar vertebra

D. If the neurological signs fail to resolve within 1 week, lumbar laminectomy and excision of any herniated nucleus pulposus should be done

Ans. B

Q 247. Acute osteomylitis is most commonly caused by:

A. Staphylococcus aureus

B. Actinomyces bovis

C. Nocardia asteroides

D. Borrelia vincentii

Ans. A

Q 248. A 45 years male presented with an expansile lesion in the centre of femoral metaphysis. The lesion shows endosteal scalloping & punctuate calcifications. Most likely diagnosis is:

A. Osteosarcoma

B. Chondrosarcoma

C. Simple bone cyst

D. Fibrous dysplasia

Ans. B

Q 249. Raju, a 10 years old child, presents with predisposition to fractures, anemia, hepatosplenomegaly and a diffusely increased radiographic density of bones. The most likely diagnosis is:

A. Osteogenesis imperfecta

B. Pyenodysotosis

C. Myelofibrosis

D. Osteopetrosis

Ans. D

Q 250. Hari Vardhman, 9 years old child, presents with scoliosis, hairy tuft in the SKIN of back and neurological deficit. Plain X-rays reveal multiple vertebral anomalies & a vertical bony spur overlying lumbar spine on AP view. The most probable diagnosis is:

A. Dorsal dermal sinus

B. Diastometamyelia

C. Tight filum terminale

D. Caudal regresion syndrome

Ans. B

Q 251. In a patient with head injury, unexplained hypotension warrants evaluation of:

A. Upper cervical spine

B. Lower cervical spine

C. Thoracic spine

D. Lumbar spine

Ans. C

Q 252. Complete transection of the spinal cord at the C1 level produces all of the following effects except:

A. Hypotension

B. Limited respiratory effort

C. Anaesthesia below the level of the lesion

D. Areflexia below the level of the lesion

Ans. B

Anaesthesia

Q 253. The gas which produces systemic toxicity without causing local irritation is:

A. Ammonia

B. Carbon monoxide

C. Hydrocyanic acid

D. Sulfur dioxide

Ans. B

Q 254. In a patient with fixed respiratory obstruction helium is used along with oxygen instead of plain oxygen because:

A. It increases oxygenation

B. It decreases turbulence

C. It decreases the dead space

D. It provides analgesia

Ans. B

Q 255. Upper respiratory tract infection is a common problem in children. All the following anesthetic complications can occur in children with respiratory infections, except:

A. Bacteremia

B. Halothane granuloma

C. Increased mucosal bleeding

D. Laryngospasm

Ans. B

Ophthalmology

Q 256. In the normal human right eye , the peripheral field of vision is usually least:

A. On the left side (nasally)

B. In the downward direction

C. In the upward direction

D. On the right side (temporally)

Ans. C

Q 257. Tonography helps you to determine:

A. The rate of formation of aqueous

B. The facilit

C. The levels of intraocular presure at different times

D. The field changes

Ans. B

Q 258. Any spectral colour can be matched by a mixture of three monochromatic lights (red, green, blue) in different proportions. If a person needs more of one of the colour for matching than a normal person, then he has a colour anomaly. More red colour is needed in the case of:

A. Deuteranomaly

B. Tritanomaly

C. Protanomaly

D. Tritanomaly

Ans. C

Q 259. The colours best appreciated by the central cones of our foveo-macular area are:

A. Red and blue

B. Blue and green

C. Red and green

D. Blue and yellow

Ans. C

Q 260. Epiphora is:

A. Cerebrospinal fluid running from the nose after FRACTURE of anterior cranial fossa

B. An epiphenomenors of a cerebral tumor

C. An abnormal overflow of tears due to obstruction of lacrimal duct

D. Eversion of lower eyelid following injury

Ans. C

Q 261. A 35 years old hypermetrope is using 1.50 D sphere both eyes. Whenever his glasses slip downward on his nose he will feel that his near vision:

A. Becomes enlarged

B. Becomes distorted

C. Becomes decreased

D. Remains the same

Ans. A

Q 262. Occulomoter nerve palsy affects all of the following muscles, except:

A. Medial rectus

B. Inferior oblique

C. Lateral rectus

D. Levetor palpabrae superioris

Ans. C

Q 263. Kusum Lata presents with acute painful red eye and mildly dilated vertically oval pupil. Most likely diagnosis is:

A. Acute retrobulbar neuritis

B. Acute angle closure glaucoma

C. Acute anterior uveitis

D. Severe keratoconjunctivitis

Ans. B

Q 264. You have been referred a midle-aged patient to rule out open angle glaucoma. Which of the following findings will help in the diagnosis:

A. Cupping of the disc

B. Depth of anterior chamber

C. Visual acuity and refractive error

D. Angle of the anterior chamber

Ans. A

Q 265. In a case of hypertensive uveitis, most useful drug to reduce intraocular pressure is:

A. Pilocarpine

B. Latanoprost

C. Physostigmine

D. Dipivefrine

Ans. B

Q 266. A patient having glaucoma develops blepharoconjunctivitis after instilling some anti-glaucoma drug. Which of the following drug can be responsible for it:

A. Timolol

B. Latanoprost

C. Dipivefrine

D. Pilocarpine

Ans. C

PART -2

ANATOMY

Q 1. The commonest variation in the arteries arising from the arch of aorta is:

A. Absence of brachiocephalic trunk.

B. Left vertebral artery arising from the arch.

C. Left common carotid artery arising from brachiocephalic trunk.

D. Presence of retroesophageal subclavian artery.

Ans. C

Q 2. The blood vessel related to the paraduodenal fossa is:

A. Gonadal vein

B. Superior mesenteric artery

C. Portal vein

D. Inferior mesenteric vein

Ans. D

Q 3. The nerve commonly damaged during McBurneys incision is:

A. Subcostal

B. Iliohypogastric

C. 11th thoracic

D. 10th thoracic

Ans. B

Q 4. The lumbar region of the vertebral column permits all the following movements, except:

A. Flexion

B. Extension

C. Lateral flexion

D. Rotation

Ans. D

Q 5. All of the following are examples of traction epiphysis, except:

A. Mastoid process

B. Tubercles of humerus

C. Trochanter of femur

D. Condyles of tibia

Ans. D

Q 6. All of the following statements are true for metaphysis of bone, except:

A. It is the strongest part of the bone.

B. It is the most vascular part of bone.

C. Growth activity is maximized here.

D. It is the region favouring hematogenous spread of infection.

Ans. A

Q 7. All of the following features can be observed after the injury to axillary nerve, except:

A. Loss of rounded contour of shoulder.

B. Loss of sensation along lateral side of upper arm.

C. Loss of overhead abduction.

D. Atrophy of deltoid muscle.

Ans. C

Q 8. All of the following muscles are grouped together as â€˜muscles of mastication, except:

A. Buccinator

B. Masseter

C. Temporalis

D. Pterygoids

Ans. A

Q 9. Referred pain from ureteric colic is felt in the groin due to involvement of the following nerve:

A. Subcostal

B. Iliohypogastric

C. Ilioinguinal

D. Genitofemoral

Ans. D

Q 10. The right coronary artery supplies all of the following parts of the conducting system in the heart, except:

A. SA Node

B. AV Node

C. AV Bundle

D. Right bundle branch

Ans. D

Q 11. The cells belonging to the following type of epithelium are provided with extra reserve of cell membrane:

A. Transitional

B. Stratified squamous

C. Stratified cuboidal

D. Stratified columnar

Ans. A

Q 12. Injury to radial nerve in lower part of spiral groove:

A. Spares nerve supply to extensor carpi radialis longus

B. Results in paralysis of anconeus muscle

C. Leaves extension at elbow joint intact

D. Weakens pronation movement

Ans. C

Q 13. A 30 year old man came to the outpatient department because he had suddenly developed double vision. On examination it was found that his right eye, when at rest, was turned medially. The most likely anatomical structures involved are:

A. Medial rectus and superior division of oculomotor nerve

B. Inferior oblique and inferior division of oculomotor nerve

C. Lateral rectus and abducent nerve

D. Superior rectus and trochlear nerve

Ans. C

Q 14. In a patient with a tumour in superior mediastinum compressing the superior vena cava, all the following veins would serve as alternate pathways for the blood to return to the right atrium, except:

A. Lateral thoracic vein

B. Internal thoracic vein

C. Hemiazygos vein

D. Vertebral venous plexus

Ans. B

Q 15. The middle cardiac vein is located at the:

A. Anterior interventricular sulcus.

B. Posterior interventricular sulcus.

C. Posterior AV groove.

D. Anterior AV groove.

Ans. B

Q 16. Which of the following statements is true about the autonomic nervous system?

A. The sympathetic outflow from the CNS is through both the cranial nerves and the sympathetic chain.

B. The parasympathetic outflow from the CNS is through cranial nerves only.

C. The superior hypogastric plexus is located at the anterior aspect of the aortic bifurcation and fifth lumbar vertebra.

D. The superior hypogastric plexus contains sympathetic fibers only.

Ans. C

PHYSIOLOGY

Q 17. An increase in which of the following parameters will shift the O2 dissociation curve to the left:

A. Temperature

B. Partial pressure of CO2

C. 2,3 DPG concentration

D. Oxygen affinity of haemoglobin

Ans. D

Q 18. A lesion of ventrolateral part of spinal cord will lead to loss (below the level of lesion) of:

A. Pain sensation on the ipsilateral side

B. Proprioception on the contralateral side

C. Pain sensation on the contralateral side

D. Proprioception on the ipsilateral side

Ans. C

Q 19. Two students, Vineet and Kamlesh were asked to demonstrate in dogs the role of sinus nerve in hypovolemic shock.Vineet severed the sinus nerve when the mean blood pressure (MBP) was 85 mm Hg and Kamlesh cut the sinus nerve when the mean blood pressure was 60 mm Hg. On cutting the sinus nerve:

A. Vineet recorded an increase in MBP but Kamlesh recorded a decrease in MBP.

B. Vineet recorded a decrease in MBP but Kamlesh recorded an increase in MBP.

C. Both recorded an increase in MBP.

D. Both recorded a decrease in MBP.

Ans. A

Q 20. As a part of space-research program, a physiologist was asked to investigate the effect of flight-induced stress on blood pressure. Accordingly the blood pressure of the cosmonauts were to be measured twice: once before the take-off, and once after the spacecraft entered the designated orbit around the earth. For a proper comparison, the preflight blood pressure should be recorded in:

A. The lying down position.

B. The sitting position.

C. The standing position

D. Any position, as long as the post-flight recording is made in the same position.

Ans. A

Q 21. The renal plasma flow (RPF) of a patient was to be estimated through the measurement of Para Amino Hippuric acid (PAH) clearance. The technician observed the procedure correctly but due to an error in the weighing inadvertently used thrice the recommended dose of PAH. The RPF estimated is likely to be:

A. False-high

B. False-low

C. False-high or false-low depending on the GFR.

D. Correct and is unaffected by the PAG overdose.

Ans. B

Q 22. The EEG record shown below is normally recordable during which stage of sleep?

A. Stage I.

B. Stage II.

C. Stage III.

D. Stage IV.

Ans. B

Q 23. Figure below represents the pH of the digestive juice aspirated from the alimentary tract as a function of position along the alimentary tract during digestion of a meal:

A. A typical value for Y2 is 9.0.

B. A typical value for Y3 is 10.0.

C. The segment C represents the pylorus.

D. The digestive enzymes active in segment A are inactivated in segment B.

Ans. D

Q 24. Which of the following statements is true for excitatory postsynaptic potentials (EPSP):

A. Are self propagating.

B. Show all or none response.

C. Are proportional to the amount of transmitter released by the presynaptic neuron.

D. Are inhibitory at presynaptic terminal.

Ans. C

Q 25. Synaptic conduction is mostly orthodromic because:

A. Dendrites cannot be depolarized.

B. Once repolarized, an area cannot be depolarized.

C. The strength of antidromic impulse is less.

D. Chemical mediator is located only in the presynaptic terminal.

Ans. D

Q 26. The cell junctions allowing exchange of cytoplasmic molecules between the two cells are called:

A. Gap junctions.

B. Tight junctions.

C. Anchoring junctions

D. Focal junctions.

Ans. A

BIOCHEMISTRY

Q 27. The main enzyme responsible for activation of xenobiotics is:

A. Cytochrome P-450

B. Glutathione S-transferase

C. NADPH cytochrome P-450-reductase

D. Glucoronyl transferase

Ans. A

Q 28. The primary defect which leads to sickle cell anemia is:

A. An abnormality in prophyrin part of hemo-globin.

B. ??

C. ??

D. Substitution of -chain of HbA.avaline by glutanmate in the

Ans. B

Q 29. Decreased glycolytic activity impairs oxygen transport by hemoglobin due to:

A. Reduced energy production

B. Decreased production of 2,3-biphospho-glycerate

C. Reduced synthesis of hemoglobin

D. Low level of oxygen

Ans. B

Q 30. The primary role of chaperones is to help in:

A. Protein synthesis

B. Protein degradation

C. Protein denaturation

D. Protein folding

Ans. D

Q 31. The conversion of an optically pure isomer (enantiomer) into a mixture of equal amounts of both dextro and levo form is called as:

A. Polymerization

B. Stereoisomerization

C. Racemization

D. Fractionation

Ans. C

Q 32. The protein rich in basic amino acids, which functions in the packaging of DNA in chromosomes, is:

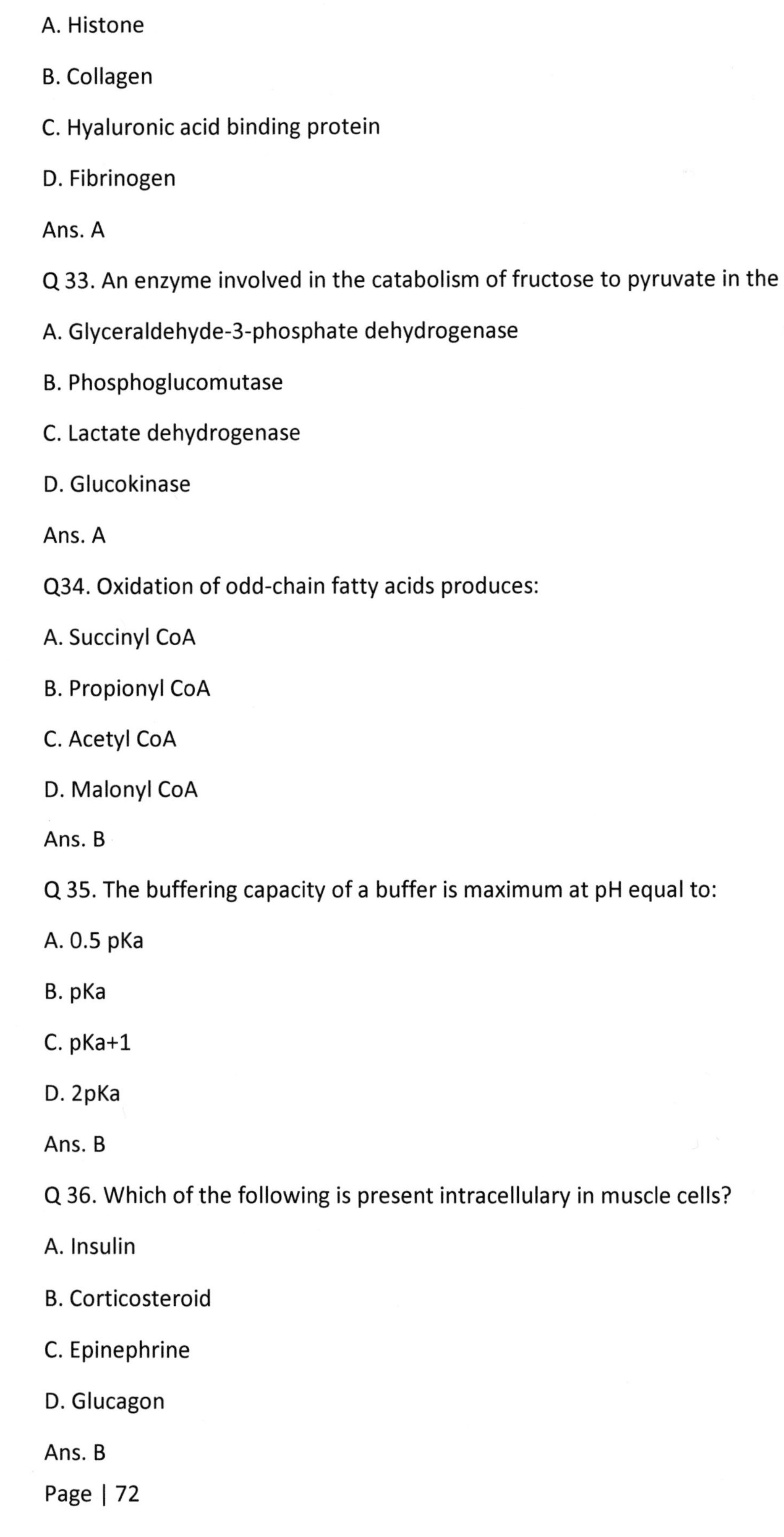

A. Histone

B. Collagen

C. Hyaluronic acid binding protein

D. Fibrinogen

Ans. A

Q 33. An enzyme involved in the catabolism of fructose to pyruvate in the liver is:

A. Glyceraldehyde-3-phosphate dehydrogenase

B. Phosphoglucomutase

C. Lactate dehydrogenase

D. Glucokinase

Ans. A

Q34. Oxidation of odd-chain fatty acids produces:

A. Succinyl CoA

B. Propionyl CoA

C. Acetyl CoA

D. Malonyl CoA

Ans. B

Q 35. The buffering capacity of a buffer is maximum at pH equal to:

A. 0.5 pKa

B. pKa

C. pKa+1

D. 2pKa

Ans. B

Q 36. Which of the following is present intracellulary in muscle cells?

A. Insulin

B. Corticosteroid

C. Epinephrine

D. Glucagon

Ans. B

Q 37. Which of the following is not a post transcriptional modification of RNA?

A. Splicing

B. 5 capping

C. 3 Polyadenylation

D. Glycosylation

Ans. D

Q 38. Serum total lactate dehydrogenase level will NOT be raised in:

A. Muscle crush injury

B. Stroke

C. Myocardial infarction

D. Hemolysis

Ans. B

Q 39. Porphobilinogen in urine produces pink colour with:

A. Fouchets reagent.

B. Benedicts reagent.

C. Sodium nitropruside.

D. Ehrlichs aldehyde reagent.

Ans. D

Q 40. The collagen triple helix structure is not found in:

A. Cytoplasm.

B. Golgi apparatus.

C. Lumen of endoplasmic reticulum.

D. Intracellular vesicles.

Ans. A

MICROBIOLOGY AND PARASITALOGY

Q 41. An anxious mother brought her 4 year old daughter to the pediatrician. The girl was passing loose bulky stools for the past 20 days. This was often associated with pain in abdomen. The pediatrician ordered the stool examination which showed the following organisms. Identify the organism:

A. Entamoeba histolytica

B. Giardia lamblia

C. Cryptosporidium

D. E. coli

Ans. B

Q 42. Heat labile instruments for use in surgical procedures can be best sterilized by:

A. Absolute alcohol

B. Ultra violet rays

C. Chlorine releasing compounds

D. Ethylene oxide gas

Ans. D

Q 43. Thirty-eight children consumed eatables procured from a picnic party. Twenty children developed abdominal cramps followed by vomiting and watery diarrhoea 6-10 hours after the party. The most likely etiology for the outbreak is:

A. Rotavirus infection

B. Entero-toxigenic E. coli infection

C. Staphylococcol toxin

D. Clostridium perfringens infection

Ans. C

Q 44. The following are true for Bordetella pertussis except:

A. It is a strict human pathogen.

B. It can be cultured from the patient during catarrhal stage.

C. It leads to invasion of the respiratory mucosa.

D. Infection can be prevented by a acellular vaccine.

Ans. C

Q 45. A chest physician performs bronchoscopy in the procedure room of the out patient department. To make the instrument safe for use in the next patient waiting outside, the most appropriate method to disinfect the endoscope is by:

A. 70% alcohol for 5 min.

B. 2% gluteraldelyde for 20 min.

C. 2% formaldehyde for 10 min.

D. 1% sodium hypochlorite for 15 min.

Ans. B

Q 46. Which of the following statements is true about rabies virus:

A. It is a double stranded RNA virus.

B. Contains a DNA-dependent RNA polymerase.

C. RNA has a negative polarity

D. Affects motor neurons.

Ans. C

Q 47. Which of the following statements is true about endemic typhus:

A. Is caused by R. rickettsii.

B. Is transmitted by the bite of fleas.

C. Has no mammalian reservoir.

D. Can be cultured in chemical defined culture medium.

Ans. B

Q 48. The organism most commonly causing genital filariasis in most parts of Bihar and eastern UP is:

A. Wuchereria bancrofti.

B. Brugia malayi.

C. Onchocerca volvulus.

D. Dirofilaria.

Ans. A

PATHOLOGY

Q 49. A married middle aged female gives history of repeated abortions for the past 5 years. The given below is conceptions prenatal karyogram. This karyogram suggests the following:

A. Klinfelters syndrome

B. Turners syndrome

C. Downs syndrome

D. Pataus syndrome

Ans. C

Q 50. An increased incidence of cholangiocarcinoma is seen in all of the following, except:

A. Hydatid cyst of liver

B. Polycystic disease of liver

C. Sclerosing cholangitis

D. Liver flukes

Ans. A

Q 51. Strong correlation with colorectal cancer is seen in:

A. Peutz-Jeghers polyp

B. Familial polyposis coli

C. Juvenile polyposis

D. Hyperplastic polyp

Ans. B

Q 52. Which of the following is the most common location of hypertensive hemorrhage?

A. Pons.

B. Thalamus.

C. Putamen/external capsule.

D. Subcortical white matter.

Ans. C

Q 53. A 63-year old man presented with massive splenomegaly, lymphadenopathy and a total leucocyte count of 17000 per mm3. The flowcytometry showed CD19 positive, CD5 positive, CD23 negative, monoclonal B-cells with bright kappa positivity comprising 80% of the peripheral blood lymphoid cells. The most likely diagnosis is:

A. Mantle cell lymphoma.

B. Splenic lymphoma with villous lymphocytes.

C. Follicular lymphoma.

D. Hairy cell leukemia.

Ans. A

Q 54. The HLA class III region genes are important elements in:

A. Transplant rejection phenomenon.

B. Governing susceptibility to autoimmune diseases.

C. Immune surveillance.

D. Antigen presentation and elimination.

Ans. C

Q 55. All the statements about lactoferrin are true, except:

A. It is present in secondary granules of neutrophil.

B. It is present in exocrine secretions of body.

C. It has great affinity for iron.

D. It transports iron for erythropoiesis.

Ans. D

Q 56. Which of the following procedures are used as routine technique for karyotyping using light microscopy?

A. C-banding B. G-banding

C. Q-banding D. Brd V-banding

Ans. B

Q 57. Restriction fragment length polymorphism is used for:

A. Analysis of chromosome structure.

B. DNA estimation.

C. Synthesis of nucleic acid.

D. Detecting proteins in a cell.

Ans. A

PHARMACOLOGY

Q 58. Granulocytopenia, gingival hyperplasia and facial hirsutism are all possible side effects of one of the following anticonvulsant drugs:

A. Phenytoin

B. Valproate

C. Carbamazepine

D. Phenobarbitone

Ans. A

Q 59. Bacitracin acts on:

A. Cell wall

B. Cell membrane

C. Nucleic acid

D. Ribosomes

Ans. A

Q 60. All of the following drugs act on cell membrane, except:

A. Nystatin

B. Griseofulvin

C. Amphotericin B

D. Polymixin B

Ans. B

Q 61. All of the following statements regarding bioavailability of a drug are true except:

A. It is the proportion (fraction) of unchanged drug that reaches the systemic circulation.

B. Bioavailability of an orally administered drug can be calculated by comparing (after oral and intravenous (IV) administration. Âµthe area under curve)

C. Low oral bioavailability always and necessarily mean poor absorption.

D. Bioavailability can be determined from plasma concentration or urinary excretion data.

Ans. C

Q 62. The extent to which ionization of a drug takes place is dependent upon pKa of the drug and the pH of the solution in which the drug is dissolved. Which of the following statements is not correct:

A. pKa of a drug is the pH at which the drug is 50% ionized.

B. Small changes of pH near the pKa of a weak acidic drug will not affect its degree of ionization.

C. Knowledge of pKa of a drug is useful in predicting its behaviour in various body fluids.

D. Phenobarbitone with a pKa of 7.2 is largely ionized at acid pH and will be about 40% non-ionised in plasma.

Ans. B

Q 63. Presence of food might be expected to interfere with drug absorption by slowing gastric emptying, or by altering the degree of ionisation of the drug in the stomach. Which of the following statement is not correct example:

A. Absorption of digoxin is delayed by the presence of food.

B. Concurrent food intake may severely reduce the rate of absorption of phenytoin.

C. Presence of food enhances the absorption of hydrochlorothiazide.

D. Antimalarial drug halofantrine is more extensively absorbed if taken with food.

Ans. B

Q 64. Bosentan is a:

A. Serotonin uptake inhibitor.

B. Endothelin receptor antagonist.

C. Leukotriene modifier.

D. Calcium sensitizer.

Ans. B

FORENSIC MEDICINE

Q 65. Mummification refers to:

A. Hardening of muscles after death

B. Colliquative putrification

C. Saponification of subcutaneous fat

D. Dessication of a dead body

Ans. D

Q 66. A patient has been allegedly bitten by cobra snake. The venom in such a bite would be:

A. Musculotoxic

B. Vasculotoxic

C. Cardiotoxic

D. Neurotoxic

Ans. D

Q 67. All the following are related to legal responsibility of an insane person except:

A. Mc Naughtens rule

B. Durhams rule

C. Currens rule

D. Rule of nine

Ans. D

Q 68. In a suspected case of death due to poisoning where cadaveric rigidity is lasting longer than usual, it may be a case of poisoning due to:

A. Lead

B. Arsenic

C. Mercury

D. Copper

Ans. B

Q 69. Blackening and tattooing of skin and clothing can be best demonstrated by:

A. Luminol spray.

B. Infrared photography.

C. Ultraviolet light.

D. Magnifying lens.

Ans. B

Q 70. Postmortem lividity is unlikely to develop in a case of:

A. Drowning in well.

B. Drowning in a fast flowing river.

C. Postmortem submersion.

D. Drowning in chlorinated swimming pool.

Ans. B

Q 71. The following situations are associated with rise of temperature after death except :

A. Burns.

B. Heat stroke.

C. Pontine hemorrhage.

D. Septicemia.

Ans. A

Q 72. In prenatal diagnostic technique Act 1994 which one of the following is not a ground for carrying out prenatal test ?

A. Pregnant women above 35 years of age.

B. History of two or more spontaneous abortion or fetal loss.

C. When fetal heart rate is 160 per min at fifth and 120 per min at ninth month.

D. History of exposure to potentially teratogenic drugs.

Ans. C

Q 73. Perjury means giving willful false evidence by a witness while under oath, the witness is liable to be prosecuted for perjury and the imprisonment may extend to seven years. This falls under which section of IPC?

A. 190 of Indian Penal Code.

B. 191 of Indian Penal Code.

C. 192 of Indian Penal Code

D. 193 of Indian Penal code.

Ans. D

Q 74. The most reliable criteria in Gustafsons method of identification is:

A. Cementum apposition.

B. Transparency of root.

C. Attrition.

D. Root resorption.

Ans. B

PREVENTIVE AND SOCIAL MEDICINE

Q 75. The parameters of sensitivity and specificity are used for assessing:

A. Criterion validity

B. Construct validity

C. Discriminant validity

D. Content validity

Ans. A

Q 76. Chi-square test is used to measure the degree of:

A. Causal relationship between exposure and effect.

B. Association between two variables.

C. Correlation between two variables.

D. Agreement between two observations.

Ans. B

Q 77. Elements of primary health care include all of the following except:

A. Adequate supply of safe water and basic sanitation.

B. Providing essential drugs.

C. Sound referral system.

D. Health education.

Ans. C

Q 78. For the calculation of positive predictive value of a screening test, the denominator is comprised of:

A. True positive + False negative

B. False positive + True negative

C. True positive + False positive

D. True positive + True negative

Ans. C

Q 79. Elemental iron and folic acid contents of pediatric iron-folic acid tablets supplied under Rural Child Health (RCH) program are:

A. 20 mg iron & 100 micrograms folic acid.

B. 40 mg iron & 100 micrograms folic acid.

C. 40 mg iron & 50 micrograms folic acid.

D. 60 mg iron & 100 micrograms folic acid.

Ans. A

Q 80. In the management of leprosy, lepromin test is most useful for:

A. Herd immunity

B. Prognosis

C. Treatment

D. Epidemiological investigations

Ans. B

Q 81. A measure of location which divides the distribution in the ratio of 3:1 is:

A. Median

B. First quartile

C. Third quartile

D. Mode

Ans. C

Q 82. The following statements about meningococcal meningitis are true, except:

A. The source of infection is mainly clinical cases.

B. The disease is more common in dry and cold months of the year.

C. Chemoprophylaxis of close contacts of cases is recommended.

D. The vaccine is not effective in children below 2 years of age.

Ans. A

Q 83. The Protein Efficiency Ratio (PER) is defined as:

A. The gain in weight of young animals per unit weight of protein-consumed.

B. The product of digestibility coeffecient and biological value.

C. The percentage of protein absorbed into the blood.

D. The percentage of nitrogen absorbed from the protein absorbed from the diet.

Ans. A

Q 84. The Vitamin A supplement administered in "Prevention of nutritional blindness in children programme" contain:

A. 25,000 i.u./ml

B. 1 lakh i.u./ml

C. 3 lakh i.u./ml

D. 5 lakh i.u./ml

Ans. B

Q 85. A 5 year old boy passed 18 loose stools in last 24 hours and vomited twice in last 4 hours. He is irritable but drinking fluids. The optimal therapy for this child is:

A. Intravenous fluids

B. Oral rehydration therapy

C. Intravenous fluid initially for 4 hours followed by oral fluids.

D. Plain water add libitum.

Ans. B

Q 86. Study this formula carefully: This denotes:

A. Sensitivity.

B. Specificity.

C. Positive Predictive value.

D. Negative Predictive value.

Ans. A

Q 87. The â€˜P value of a randomized controlled trial comparing operation A (new procedure) and operation B (Gold standard is 0.04). From this, we conclude that:

A. Type II error is small and we can accept the findings of the study.

B. The probability of false negative conclusion that operation A is better than operation B, when in truth it is not, is 4%.

C. The power of study to detect a difference between operation A and B is 96%.

D. The probability of a false positive conclusion that operation A is better than operation B, when in truth it is not, is 4%.

Ans. D

Q 88. The commonest cause of low vision in India is:

A. Uncorrected refractive error

B. Cataract.

C. Glaucoma

D. Squint.

Ans. A

Q 89. Most important epidemiological tool used for assessing disability in children is:

A. Activities of Daily Living (ADL) scale.

B. Wings Handicaps, Behaviour and Skills (HBS) Schedule.

C. Binet and Simon IQ tests.

D. Physical Quality of Life Index (PQLI).

Ans. B

Q 90. Scope of family planning services include all of the following except:

A. Screening for cervical cancer.

B. Providing services for unmarried mothers.

C. Screening for HIV infection.

D. Providing adoption services.

Ans. C

Q 91. Class II exposure in animal bites includes the following:

A. Scratches without oozing of blood.

B. Licks on a fresh wound.

C. Scratch with oozing of blood on palm.

D. Bites from wild animals.

Ans. B

Q 92. Elemental iron and folic acid contents of iron and folic acid adult tablets supplied under the "National Programme for Anaemia Prophylaxis" are:

A. 60 mg of elemental iron and 250 microgram of folic acid.

B. 100 mg of elemental iron and 500 micrograms of folic acid.

C. 20 mg of elemental iron and 750 micrograms of folic acid.

D. 200 mg of elemental iron and 1000 micro-grams of folic acid.

Ans. B

Q 93. Denominator while calculating the secondary attack rate includes:

A. All the people living in next fifty houses.

B. All the close contacts.

C. All susceptibles amongst close contact.

D. All susceptibles in the whole village.

Ans. C

Q 94. The response which is graded by an observer on an agree or disagree continuum is based on:

A. Visual analog scale.

B. Guttman scale.

C. Likert scale.

D. Adjectival scale.

Ans. C

Q 95. For calculation of sample size for a prevalence study all of the following are necessary except:

A. Prevalence of disease in population.

B. Power of the study.

C. Significance level.

D. Desired precision.

Ans. D

Q 96. Leprosy is considered a public health problem if the prevalence of leprosy is more than:

A. 1 per 10,000

B. 2 per 10,000

C. 5 per 10,000

D. 10 per 10,000

Ans. A

Q 97. For controlling an outbreak of cholera, all of the following measures are recommended except:

A. Mass chemoprophylaxis.

B. Proper disposal of excreta.

C. Chlorination of water.

D. Early detection and management of cases.

Ans. A

Q 98. A child aged 24 months was brought to the Primary Health Centre with complaints of cough and fever for the past 2 days. On examination, the child weighed 11 kg., respiratory rate was 38 per minute, chest indrawing was present. The most appropriate line of management for this patient is?

A. Classify as pneumonia and refer urgently to secondary level hospital.

B. Classify as pneumonia, start antibiotics and advise to report after 2 days.

C. Classify as severe pneumonia, start antibiotics and refer urgently.

D. Classify as severe pneumonia and refer urgently.

Ans. C

MEDICINE

Q 99. The syndromic management of urethral discharge includes treatment of:

A. Neisseria gonorrhoeae and herpes genitalis.

B. Chlamydia trachomatis and herpes genitalis.

C. Neisseria gonorrhoeae and Chlamydia trachomatis.

D. Syphilis and chancroid.

Ans. C

Q 100. A 56 year old man presents in the casualty with severe chest pain and difficulty in breathing. His ECG was taken immediately. The above ECG suggest the following diagnosis:

A. Ventricular fibrillation

B. Acute pulmonary embolism

C. Second degree heart block

D. Atrial fibrillation

Ans. B

Q 101. All of the following infections are often associated with acute intravascular hemolysis except:

A. Clostridium tetani

B. Bartonella bacilliformis

C. Plasmodium falciparum

D. Babesia microti

Ans. A

Q 102. All of the following are the electrocardiographic features of severe hyperkalemia except:

A. Peaked T waves

B. Presence of U waves

C. Sine wave pattern

D. Loss of P waves

Ans. B

Q 103. The correct sequence of cell cycle is:

A. G0 -G1 -S -G2 -M

B. G0 -G1 -G2 -S -M

C. G0 -M -G2 -S -G1

D. G0 -G1 -S -M -G2

Ans. A

Q 104. Commonest cause of sporadic encephalitis is:

A. Japanese B Virus

B. Herpes Simplex Virus

C. Human Immunodeficiency Virus

D. Rubeola Virus

Ans. B

Q 105. Raised serum level of lipoprotein -(a) is a predictor of:

A. Cirrhosis of liver

B. Rheumatic arthritis

C. Atherosclerosis

D. Cervical cancer

Ans. C

Q 106. Haemorrhage secondary to heparin administration can be best corrected by administration of:

A. Vitamin K

B. Whole blood

C. Protamine

D. Ascorbic acid

Ans. C

Q 107. Which one of the following conditions may lead to exudative pleural effusion:

A. Cirrhosis

B. Nephrotic syndrome

C. Congestive heart failure

D. Bronchogenic carcinoma

Ans. D

Q 108. A 60 year old man is diagnosed to be suffering from Legionnaires disease after he returns home from attending a convention. He could have acquired it:

A. From a person suffering from the infection while travelling in the aeroplane.

B. From a chronic carrier in the convention center.

C. From inhalation of the aerosol in the air-conditioned room at convention center.

D. By sharing an infected towel with a fellow delegate at the convention.

Ans. C

Q 109. In a post-operative intensive care unit, five patients developed post-operative wound infection on the same day. The best method to prevent cross infection occurring in other patients in the same ward is to:

A. Give antibiotics to all other patients in the ward.

B. Fumigate the ward.

C. Disinfect the ward with sodium hypochlorite.

D. Practice proper hand washing.

Ans. D

Q 110. The earliest immunoglobulin to be synthesized by the fetus is:

A. IgA

B. IgG

C. IgE

D. IgM

Ans. D

Q 111. The following are true regarding Lymes disease, except:

A. It is transmitted by Ixodes tick.

B. Erythema chronicum migrans may be a clinical feature.

C. Borrelia recurrentis is the aetiological agent.

D. Rodents act as natural hosts.

Ans. C

Q 112. A couple, with a family history of beta thalassemia major in a distant relative, has come for counselling. The husband has HbA2 of 4.8% and the wife has HbA2 of 2.3%. The risk of having a child with beta thalassemia major is:

A. 50%

B. 25%

C. 5%

D. 0%

Ans. D

Q 113. A 2 month old baby with acute icteric viral hepatitis like illness slips into encephalopathy after 48 hours. The mother is a known hepatitis B carrier. Mothers hepatitis B virus serological profile is most likely to be:

A. HBsAg positive only

B. HBsAg and HBeAg positive

C. HBsAg and HBe antibody positive

D. HBV DNA positive

Ans. C

Q 114. A 7 year old girl from Bihar presented with three episodes of massive hematemesis and melena. There is no history of jaundice. On examination, she had a large spleen, non-palpable liver and mild ascites. Portal vein was not visualised on ultrasonography. Liver function tests were normal and endoscopy revealed esophageal varices. The most likely diagnosis is:

A. Kala azar with portal hypertension

B. Portal hypertension of unknown etiology

C. Chronic liver disease with portal hypertension

D. Portal hypertension due to extrahepatic obstruction.

Ans. D

Q 115. A 40 year old male had undergone splenectomy 20 years ago. Peripheral blood smear examination would show the presence of:

A. Dohle bodies

B. Hypersegmented neutrophils

C. Spherocytes

D. Howell-Jolly bodies

Ans. D

Q 116. Which of the heart valve is most likely to be involved by infective endocarditis following a septic abortion?

A. Aortic valve

B. Tricuspid valve

C. Pulmonary valve

D. Mitral valve

Ans. B

Q 117. Central nervous system manifestations in chronic renal failure are a result of all of the following, except:

A. Hyperosmolarity

B. Hypocalcemia

C. Acidosis

D. Hyponatremia

Ans. A

Q 118. Medullary carcinoma of the thyroid is associated with which of the following syndrome:

A. MEN I

B. MEN II

C. Fraumeni syndrome

D. Hashimotos syndrome

Ans. B

Q 119. Which of the following statements represent most correct interpretation from the ECG waveform given below:

A. X-originated from an atrial ectopic focus.

B. X reset the cardiac rhythm.

C. Both heart sounds would have been present at X beat.

D. The path of spread of excitation was normal.

Ans. B

Q 120. A 60 year old male presented to the emergency with breathlessness, facial swelling and dilated veins on the chest wall. The most common cause is:

A. Thymoma.

B. Lung cancer.

C. Hodgkins lymphoma.

D. Superior vena caval obstruction.

Ans. B

Q 121. All of the following conditions may predispose to pulmonary embolism except:

A. Protein S deficiency.

B. Malignancy.

C. Obesity.

D. Progesterone therapy.

Ans. D

Q 122. An early systolic murmur may be caused by all of the following except:

A. Small ventricular septal defect.

B. Papillary muscle dysfunction.

C. Tricuspid regurgitation.

D. Aortic stenosis.

Ans. D

Q 123. Troponin-T is preferable to CPK-MB in the diagnosis of acute myocardial infarction (MI) in all of the following situations except:

A. Bedside diagnosis of MI.

B. Postoperatively (after CABG).

C. Reinfarction after 4 days.

D. Small infarcts.

Ans. C

Q 124. The most common cause of tricuspid regurgitation is secondary to:

A. Rheumatic heart disease.

B. Dilatation of right ventricle.

C. Coronary artery disease.

D. Endocarditis due to intravenous drug abuse.

Ans. B

Q 125. Absence seizures are characterized on EEG by:

A. 3 Hz spike & wave

B. 1-2 Hz spike & wave.

C. Generalized polyspikes.

D. Hypsarrythmia.

Ans. A

Q 126. All of the following are associated with low C3 levels except:

A. Post streptococcal glomerulonephritis.

B. Membrano-proliferative glomerulonephritis.

C. Goodpastures disease.

D. Systemic lupus erythematosus.

Ans. C

Q 127. Normal anion gap metabolic acidosis is caused by:

A. Cholera.

B. Starvation.

C. Ethylene glycol poisoning.

D. Lactic acidosis.

Ans. A

Q 128. Diagnostic features of allergic broncho-pulmonary aspergillosis (ABPA) include all of the following except:

A. Changing pulmonary infiltrates.

B. Peripheral eosinophilia.

C. Serum precipitins against Aspergillous fumigatus.

D. Occurrence in patients with old cavitary lesions.

Ans. D

Q 129. The syndrome of inappropriate antidiuretic hormone is characterized by the following:

A. Hyponatremia and urine sodium excretion > 20 mEq/l.

B. Hypernatremia and urine sodium excretion > 20 mEq/l.

C. Hyponatremia and hyperkalemia.

D. Hypernatremia and hypokalemia.

Ans. A

Q 130. All of the following heart sounds occur shortly after S2 except:

A. Opening snap.

B. Pericardial knock.

C. Ejection click.

D. Tumor plop.

Ans. C

Q 131. Pulmonary hypertension may occur in all of the following conditions except:

A. Toxic oil syndrome.

B. Progressive systemic sclerosis.

C. Sickle cell anaemia.

D. Argemone mexicana poisoning.

Ans. D

Q 132. Causes of metabolic alkalosis include all the following, except:

A. Mineralocorticoid deficiency.

B. Bartters syndrome.

C. Thiazide diuretic therapy.

D. Recurrent vomiting.

Ans. A

Q 133. The most frequent cause of recurrent genital ulceration in a sexually active male is:

A. Herpes genitalis.

B. Aphthous ulcer.

C. Syphilis.

D. Chancroid.

Ans. A

Q 134. The most effective drug against M. leprae is:

A. Dapsone.

B. Rifampicin.

C. Clofazimine.

D. Prothionamide.

Ans. B

Q 135. A 30-year old HIV positive patient presents with fever, dyspnoea and non-productive cough, patient is cyanosed. His chest X-ray reveals bilateral, symmetrical interstitial infiltrates. The most likely diagnosis is:

A. Tuberculosis.

B. Cryptococcosis.

C. Pneunocystis carinii pneumonia.

D. Toxoplasmosis.

Ans. C

Q 136. Extensive pleural thickening and calcification especially involving the diaphragmatic pleura are classical features of:

A. Coal workers pneumoconiosis.

B. Asbestosis.

C. Silicosis.

D. Siderosis.

Ans. B

Q 137. Commonest presentation of neurocysticercosis is:

A. Seizures.

B. Focal neurological deficits.

C. Dementia

D. Radiculopathy.

Ans. A

Q 138. A 55-year old man who has been on bed rest for the past 10 days, complains of breathlessness and chest pain. The chest X-ray is normal. The next investigation should be:

A. Lung ventilation-perfusion scan.

B. Pulmonary arteriography.

C. Pulmonary venous angiography.

D. Echocardiography.

Ans. B

Q 139. A 60-year old man with diabetes mellitus presents with painless, swollen right ankle joint. Radiograph of the ankle shows destroyed joint with large number of loose bodies. The most probable diagnosis is:

A. Charcots joint

B. Cluttons joint

C. Osteoarthritis.

D. Rheumatoid arthritis.

Ans. A

Q 140. All of the following statements regarding the ECG in acute pericarditis are true except:

A. T wave inversion develop before ST elevations return to baseline.

B. Global ST segment elevation is seen in early pericarditis.

C. Sinus tachycardia is a common finding.

D. PR segment depression is present in majority of patients.

Ans. A

Q 141. Type IV hypersensitivity to Mycobacterium tuberculosis antigen may manifest as:

A. Iridocyclitis.

B. Polyarteritis nodosa.

C. Phlyctenular conjunctivitis.

D. Giant cell arteritis.

Ans. C

Q 142. The blood gas parameters: pH 7.58, pCO2 23 mmHg, PO2 300 mmHg and oxygen saturation 60% are most consistent with:

A. Carbon monoxide poisoning.

B. Ventilatory malfunction.

C. Voluntary hyperventilation.

D. Methyl alcohol poisoning.

Ans. A

Q 143. Most suitable radioisotope of iodine for treating hyperthyroidism is:

A. I123

B. I125

C. I131

D. I132

Ans. C

Q 144. In the presence of vasopressin the greatest fraction of filtered water is reabsorbed in which part of the nephron:

A. Proximal tubule.

B. Distal tubule.

C. Loope of Henle.

D. Collecting duct.

Ans. A

Q 145. All of the following statements are correct about potassium balance, except:

A. Most of potassium is intracellular.

B. Three quarter of the total body potassium is found in skeletal muscle.

C. Intracellular potassium is released into extra-cellular space in response to severe injury.

D. Acidosis leads to movement of potassium from extracellular to intracellular fluid compartment.

Ans. D

Q 146. Hypocalcemia is characterized by all of the following features except:

A. Numbness and tingling of circumoral region.

B. Hyperactive tendon reflexes.

C. Shortening of Q-T interval in ECG.

D. Carpopedal spasm.

Ans. C

Q 147. Which of the following is not true about Bergers disease?

A. The pathologic changes are proliferation and usually confined to mesangial cells; usually focal and segmental.

B. Hematuria may be gross or microscopic.

C. On immunoflurorescence deposits contain both IgA and IgG.

D. Absence of associated proteinuria is pathognomonic.

Ans. D

Q 148. All of the following are risk factors for deep vein thrombosis (DVT) except:

A. Duration of surgery more than thirty minutes.

B. Obesity.

C. Age less than forty years.

D. Use of the oestrogen-progesterone contraceptive pills.

Ans. C

Q 149. A labourer involved with repair-work of sewers was admitted with fever, jaundice and renal failure. The most appropriate test to diagnose the infection in this patient is:

A. Weil Felix test.

B. Paul Bunnel test.

C. Microscopic agglutination test.

D. Micro immunofluorescence test.

Ans. C

Q 150. Memory T cells can be identified by using the following marker:

A. CD45 RA.

B. CD45 RB.

C. CD45 RC.

D. CD45 RO.

Ans. D

Q 151. All of the following statements about NK cells are true, except:

A. They are derived from large granular cells.

B. They comprise about 5% of human peripheral lymphoid cells.

C. They are MHC restricted cytotoxic cells.

D. They express IgG Fc receptors.

Ans. C

Q 152. Which of the following increases the susceptibility to coronary artery disease:

A. Type V hyperlipoproteinaemia.

B. Von Willebrandts disease.

C. Nephrotic syndrome.

D. Systemic lupus erythematosus.

Ans. D

Q 153. MHC class III genes encode:

A. Complement component C3.

B. Tumor necrosis factor.

C. Interleukin 2.

D. Beta 2 microglobulin.

Ans. B

Q 154. Gluten sensitive enteropathy is most strongly associated with:

A. HLA-DQ2.

B. HLA-DR4.

C. HLA-DQ3.

D. Blood group â€˜B.

Ans. A

Q 155. Most sensitive and specific test for diagnosis of iron deficiency is:

A. Serum iron levels.

B. Serum ferritin levels.

C. Serum transferrin receptor population.

D. Transferrin saturation.

Ans. B

Q 156. All of the following are poor prognostic factors for acute myeloid leukemias, except:

A. Age more than 60 years.

B. Leucocyte count more than 1,00,000/Âµl.

C. Secondary leukemias.

D. Presence of t(8;21).

Ans. D

Q 157. Leukoerythroblastic picture may be seen in all of the following, except:

A. Myelofibrosis.

B. Metastatic carcinoma.

C. Gauchers disease.

D. Thalassemia.

Ans. D

Q 158. Cardiac or central nervous system toxicity may result when standard lidocaine doses are administered to patients with circulatory failure. This may be due to the following reason:

A. Lidocaine concentration are initially higher in relatively well perfused tissues such as brain and heart.

B. Histamine receptors in brain and heart gets suddenly activated in circulatory failure.

C. There is a sudden out-bursts of release of adrenaline, noradrenaline and dopamine in brain and heart.

D. Lidocaine is converted into a toxic metabolite due to its longer stay in liver.

Ans. A

Q 159. All of the following are useful intravenous therapy for hypertensive emergencies, except:

A. Fenoldopam.

B. Urapidil.

C. Enalapril.

D. Nifedipine.

Ans. D

Q 160. Cardiac output measured by thermodilution technique is unreliable in all of the following situations except:

A. Ventricular septal defect.

B. Tricuspid regurgitation.

C. Low cardiac output.

D. Pulmonary regurgitation.

Ans. A

Q 161. Exercise testing is absolutely contraindi-cated in which one of the following:

A. One week following myocardial infarction.

B. Unstable angina.

C. Aortic stenosis.

D. Peripheral vascular disease.

Ans. B

Q 162. A nineteen year old female with short stature, wide spread nipples and primary amenorrhoea most likely has a karyotype of:

A. 47, XX+18.

B. 46, XXY.

C. 47, XXY.

D. 45 X.

Ans. D

Q 163. Osteomalacia is associated with:

A. Decrease in osteoid volume.

B. Decrease in osteoid surface.

C. Increase in osteoid maturation time.

D. Increase in mineral apposition rate.

Ans. C

Q 164. A 23-year old woman has experienced episodes of myalgias, pleural effusion, pericarditis and arthralgias without joint deformity over course of several years. The best laboratory screening test to diagnose her disease would be:

A. CD4 lymphocyte count.

B. Erythrocyte sedimentation rate.

C. Antinuclear antibody.

D. Assay for thyroid hormones.

Ans. C

Q 165. A 5-year old boy is detected to be HBsAg positive on two separate occasions during a screening program for hepatitis B. He is otherwise asymptomatic. Child was given 3 doses of recombinant hepatitis B vaccine at the age of one year. His mother was treated for chronic hepatitis B infection around the same time. The next relevant step for further investigating the child would be to:

A. Obtain HBe Ag and anti-HBe antibodies.

B. Obtain anti-HBs levels.

C. Repeat HBsAg.

D. Repeat another course of hepatitis B vaccine.

Ans. A

Q 166. Which of the following hepatitis viruses have significant perinatal transmission:

A. Hepatitis E virus.

B. Hepatitis C virus

C. Hepatitis B virus.

D. Hepatitis A virus.

Ans. C

Q 167. The diffusion capacity of lung (DLCO) is decreased in all of the following conditions except:

A. Interstitial lung disease.

B. Goodpastures syndrome.

C. Emphysema.

D. Primary pulmonary hypertension.

Ans. B

Q 168. Oslers nodes are typically seen in which one of the following:

A. Chronic candida endocarditis.

B. Acute staphylococcal endocarditis.

C. Pseudomonas endocarditis.

D. Libman sacks endocarditis.

Ans. B

Q 169. Thiamine deficiency is known to occur in all of the following except:

A. Food Faddist.

B. Homocystinemia

C. Chronic alcoholic

D. Chronic heart failure patients on diuretics.

Ans. B

Q 170. Radiation exposure during infancy has been linked to which one of the following carcinoma:

A. Breast.

B. Melanoma.

C. Thyroid.

D. Lung.

Ans. C

Q 171. Recurrent ischemic events following thrombolysis has been pathophysiologically linked to which of the following factors:

A. Antibodies to thrombolytic agents.

B. Fibrinopeptide A.

C. Lipoprotein (a) [Lp(a)].

D. Triglycerides.

Ans. A

Q 172. Which of the following is pan-T lymphocyte marker?

A. CD2.

B. CD3.

C. CD19.

D. CD25

Ans. B

Q 173. Following are the features of corticospinal involvement except:

A. Cog-wheel rigidity.

B. Spasticity.

C. Plantar extensor response.

D. Exaggerated deep tendon reflexes.

Ans. A

Q 174. Positive feedback action of estrogen for inducting luteinizing hormone surge is associated with one of the following steroid hormone ratios in peripheral circulation:

A. High estrogen : low progesterone.

B. Low estrogen : high progesterone.

C. Low estrogen : low progestrone

D. High estrogen : high progesterone.

Ans. A

Q 175. A post-operative cardiac surgical patient developed sudden hypotension, raised central venous pressure, pulsus paradoxus at the 4th post operative hour. The most probable diagnosis is:

A. Excessive mediastinal bleeding.

B. Ventricular dysfunction.

C. Congestive cardiac failure.

D. Cardiac tamponade.

Ans. D

PEDIATRICS

Q 176. All of the following may occur in Noonans syndrome except:

A. Hypertrophic cardiomyopathy.

B. Cryptorchidism.

C. Infertility in females.

D. Autosomal dominant transmission.

Ans. C

Q 177. In an single visit, a 9-month old, unimmunized child can be given the following vaccination:

A. Only BCG.

B. BCG, DPT-1, OPV-1.

C. DPT-1, OPV-1, Measles.

D. BCG, DPT-1 OPV-1, Measles.

Ans. D

Q 178. An eight-year old boy had abdominal pain, fever with bloody diarrhea for 18 months. His height is 110 cms and weight is 14.5 kg. Stool culture was negative for known enteropathogens. The sigmoidoscopy was normal. During the same period, child had an episode of renal colic and passed urinary gravel. The mantoux test was 5 Ã— 5 mm. The most probable diagnosis is:

A. Ulcerative colitis.

B. Crohns disease.

C. Intestinal tuberculosis.

D. Strongyloidosis.

Ans. B

Q 179. A 45-day old infant developed icterus and two days later symptoms and signs of acute liver failure appeared. Child was found to be positive for HBsAg. The mother was also HBs Ag carrier. The mothers hepatitis B serological profile is likely to be:

A. HBsAg positive only.

B. HBsAg and HbeAg positivity.

C. HBsAg and anti-HBe antibody positivity.

D. Mother infected with mutant HBV.

Ans. B

Q 180. A 15-year old healthy boy with no major medical problem complaints that he breaks out with blocky areas of erythema that are pruritic over skin of his arm, leg and trunk every time within an hour of eating sea foods. The clinical features are suggestive of:

A. Localised immune-complex deposition.

B. Cell mediated hypersensitivity.

C. Localized anaphylaxis.

D. Release of complement C3b.

Ans. C

Q 181. A 2-month baby presents with history of jaundice, turmeric colored urine and pale stools since birth. Examination reveals liver span of 10 cms, firm in consistency and spleen of 3 cms. The most specific investigation for establishing the diagnosis would be:

A. Liver function tests.

B. Ultrasound abdomen.

C. Peroperative cholangiogram.

D. Liver biopsy.

Ans. D

Q 182. Transient myeloproliferative disorder of the newborn is seen in association with:

A. Turner syndrome.

B. Down syndrome.

C. Neurofibromatosis.

D. Ataxia telangiectasia.

Ans. B

Q 183. A 1-month old baby presents with frequent vomiting and failure to thrive. There are features of moderate dehydration. Blood sodium is 122 mEq/l and potassium is 6.1 mEq/l. The most likely diagnosis is:

A. Gitelman syndrome.

B. Bartter Syndrome

C. 21-hydroxylase deficiency.

D. 11-hydroxylase deficiency

Ans. C

Q 184. A male child of 15 years, with a mental age of 9 years has an IQ of:

A. 50

B. 60

C. 70

D. 80

Ans. B

Q 185. The most appropriate drug used for chelation therapy in beta thalassemia major is:

A. Oral desferrioxamine.

B. Oral deferiprone.

C. Intramuscular EDTA.

D. Oral Succimer.

Ans. B

Q 186. Which endocrine disorder is associated with epiphyseal dysgenesis ?

A. Hypothyroidism.

B. Cushings syndrome.

C. Addisons disease.

D. Hypoparathyroidism.

Ans. A

Q 187. An albino girl gets married to a normal boy. What are the chances of their having an affected child and what are the chances of their children being carriers?

A. None affected, all carriers.

B. All normal.

C. 50% carriers.

D. 50% affected, 50% carriers.

Ans. A

Q 188. Which one of the following statements is false with regard to Xanthogranulomatous pyelonephritis in children.

A. Often affects those younger than 8 years of age.

B. It affects the kidney focally more frequently than diffusely.

C. Boys are affected more frequently.

D. Clinical presentation in children is same as in adults.

Ans. D

Q 189. Which one of the following statements is false with regard to pyuria in children?

A. Presence of more than 5 WBC/hpf (high power field) for girls and more than 3 WBC/hpf for boys.

B. Infection can occur without pyuria.

C. Pyuria may be present without urinary tract infection.

D. Isolated pyuria is neither confirmatory nor diagnostic for urinary tract infection.

Ans. D

Q 190. Which one of the following is the most common cause of abdominal mass in neonates?

A. Neuroblastoma.

B. Wilms tumour.

C. Distended bladder.

D. Multicystic dysplastic kidneys.

Ans. D

DERMATOLOGY

Q 191. Acantholysis is characterstic of:

A. Pemphigus vulgaris

B. Pemphigoid

C. Erythema multiforme

D. Dermatitis herpetiformis

Ans. A

Q 192. A 5 year old boy has multiple asymptomatic oval and circular faintly hypopigmented macules with scaling on his face. The most probable clinical diagnosis is:

A. Pityriasis versicolor.

B. Indeterminate leprosy.

C. Pityriasis alba.

D. Acrofacial vitiligo.

Ans. C

Q 193. A 40-year old male developed persistent oral ulcers followed by multiple flaccid bullae on trunk and extremities. Direct examination of a skin biopsy immunofluorescence showed intercellular IgG deposits in the epidermis. The most

probable diagnosis is:

A. Pemphigus vulgaris.

B. Bullous pemphigoid.

C. Bullous lupus erythematosus.

D. Epidermolysis bullosa acquisita.

Ans. A

Q 194. The test likely to help in diagnosis of a patient who presents with an itchy annular plaque on the face is:

A. Grams stain.

B. Potassium hydroxide mount.

C. Tissue smear.

D. Woods lamp examination.

Ans. B

Q 195. An eleven year old boy is having tinea capitis on his scalp. The most appropriate line of treatment is:

A. Oral griseofulvin therapy.

B. Topical griseofulvin therapy.

C. Shaving of the scalp.

D. Selenium sulphide shampoo.

Ans. A

Q 196. An 8 month old child presented with itchy, exudative lesions on the face, palms and soles. The sibling also have similar com-plaints. The treatment of choice in such a patient is:

A. Systemic ampicillin.

B. Topical betamethasone.

C. Systemic prednisolone.

D. Topical permethrin.

Ans. D

Q 197. Which of the following symbol represent adopted individuals:

A.

B.

C.

D.

Ans. D

Q 198. All of the following are features of hallucinations, except:

A. It is independent of the will of the observer.

B. Sensory organs are not involved.

C. It is as vivid as that in a true sense perception.

D. It occurs in the absence of a perceptual stimulus.

Ans. B

Q 199. Delirium tremens is characterized by confusion associated with:

A. Autonomic hyperactivity and tremors.

B. Features of intoxication due to alcohol.

C. Sixth nerve palsy.

D. Korsakoff psychosis.

Ans. A

Q 200. All of the following are impulse control disorders except:

A. Pyromania.

B. Trichotillomania.

C. Kleptomania.

D. Capgras syndrome.

Ans. D

Q 201. A 20-year old man has presented with increased alcohol consumption and sexual indulgence, irritability, lack of sleep and not feeling fatigued even on prolonged periods of activity. All these changes have been present for 3 weeks. The most likely diagnosis is:

A. Alcohol dependence.

B. Schizophrenia.

C. Mania.

D. Impulsive control disorder.

Ans. C

Q 202. An alcoholic is brought to the Emergency OPD with the complaint of irrelevant talking. He had stopped using alcohol three days back. On examination, he is found to be disoriented to time, place and person. He also has visual illusions and hallucinations. There is no history of head injury. The most likely diagnosis is:

A. Dementia praecox.

B. Derlirium tremens.

C. Schizophrenia.

D. Korsakoffs psychosis.

Ans. B

Q 203. A 41-year old married female presented with headache for the last 6 months. She had several consultations. All her investigations were found to be within normal limits. She still insists that there is something wrong in her head and seeks another consultation. The most likely diagnosis is:

A. Phobia.

B. Psychogenic headache.

C. Hypochondriasis.

D. Depression.

Ans. C

Q 204. Behavior therapy to change maladaptive behaviors using response as reinforcer uses the principles of:

A. Classical conditioning.

B. Moneling.

C. Social learning.

D. Operant conditioning.

Ans. D

Q 205. A 15 year old boy feels that the dirt has hung onto him whenever he passes through the dirty street. This repetitive thought causes much distress and anxiety. He knows that there is actually no such thing after he has cleaned once but he is not satisfied and is compelled to think so. This has led to social withdrawal. He spends much of his time thinking about the dirt and contamination. This has affected his studies also. The most likely diagnosis is:

A. Obsessive compulsive disorder.

B. Conduct disorder.

C. Agoraphobia.

D. Adjustment disorder.

Ans. A

Q 206. A 50 year old man has presented with pain in back, lack of interest in recreational activities, low mood, lethargy, decreased sleep and appetite for two months. There was no history suggestive of delusions or hallucinations. He did not suffer from any chronic medical illness. There was no family history of psychiatric illness. Routine investigations including haemogram, renal function tests, liver functions tests, electrocardiogram did not reveal any abnormality. This patient should be treated with:

A. Haloperidol.

B. Sertraline.

C. Alprazolam.

D. Olanzapine.

Ans. B

GENERAL SURGERY

Q 207. A 70 year old male patient presented with history of chest pain and was diagnosed to have coronary artery disease. During routine evaluation, an ultrasound of the abdomen showed presence of gallbladder stones. There was no past history of biliary colic or jaundice. What is the best treatment advice for such a patient for his gallbladder stones:

A. Open cholecystectomy

B. Laparoscopic cholecystectomy

C. No surgery for gallbladder stones

D. ERCP and removal of gallbladder stones

Ans. C

Q 208. Early stage of trauma is characterized by:

A. Catabolism.

B. Anabolism.

C. Glycogenesis.

D. Gluconeogenesis.

Ans. A

Q 209. Bedsore is an example of:

A. Tropical ulcer

B. Trophic ulcer

C. Venous ulcer

D. Post thrombotic ulcer

Ans. B

Q 210. Marjolins ulcer is:

A. Malignant ulcer found on the scar of burn.

B. Malignant ulcer found on infected foot.

C. Trophic ulcer.

D. Meleneys gangrene.

Ans. A

Q 211. If a patient with Raynauds disease immer-sed his hand in cold water, the hand will:

A. Become red.

B. Remain unchanged.

C. Turn white.

D. Become blue.

Ans. C

Q 212. The best treatment for cystic hygroma is:

A. Surgical excision.

B. Radiotherapy.

C. Sclerotherapy.

D. Chemotherapy.

Ans. A

Q 213. Which of the following is most suggestive of neonatal small bowel obstruction:

A. Generalised abdominal distension.

B. Failure to pass meconeum in the first 24 hours.

C. Bilious vomiting.

D. Refusal of feeds.

Ans. C

Q 214. What is most characteristic of congenital hypertrophic pyloric stenosis:

A. Affects the first born female child.

B. The pyloric tumour is best felt during feeding.

C. The patient is commonly marasmic.

D. Loss of appetite occurs early.

Ans. B

Q 215. Which of the following lasers is used for treatment of benign prostatic hyperplasia as well as urinary calculi?

A. CO2 laser

B. Excimer laser

C. Ho : YAG laser

D. Nd : YAG laser

Ans. C

Q 216. What is the most appropriate operation for a solitary nodule in one lobe of thyroid?

A. Lobectomy

B. Hemithyroidectomy.

C. Nodule removal.

D. Partial lobectomy with 1 cm margin around nodule.

Ans. B

Q 217. A posteriorly perforating ulcer in the pyloric antrum of the stomach is most likely to produce initial localized peritonitis or abscess formation in the following:

A. Omental bursa (lesser sac)

B. Greater sac

C. Right subphrenic space

D. Hepatorenal space (pouch of Morrison)

Ans. A

Q 218. A 65-year old male smoker presents with gross total painless hematuria. The most likely diagnosis is:

A. Carcinoma urinary bladder.

B. Benign prostatic hyperplasia.

C. Carcinoma prostate.

D. Cystolithiasis.

Ans. A

Q 219. A 10-mm calculus in the right lower ureter associated with proximal hydrouretero-nephrosis is best treated with:

A. Extracorporeal shockwave lithotripsy.

B. Antegrade percutaneous access.

C. Open ureterolithotomy.

D. Ureteroscopic retrieval.

Ans. D

Q 220. Semen analysis of a young man who presented with primary infertility revealed low volume, fructose negative ejaculate with azoospermia. Which of the following is the most useful imaging modality to evaluate the cause of his infertility ?

A. Colour duplex ultrasonography of the scrotum.

B. Transrectal ultrasonography.

C. Retrograde urethrography

D. Spermatic venography.

Ans. B

Q 221. A 70 year old patient with benign prostatic hyperplasia underwent transurethral resection of prostate under spinal anaesthesia. One hour later, he developed vomiting and altered sensorium. the most probable cause is:

A. Overdosage of spinal anaesthetic agent.

B. Rupture of bladder.

C. Hyperkalemia.

D. Water intoxication.

Ans. D

Q 222. A 50-year old male, working as a hotel cook, has four dependent family members. He has been diagnosed with an early stage squamous cell cancer of anal canal. He has more than 60% chances of cure. The best treatment option is:

A. Abdomino-perineal resection.

B. Combined surgery and radiotherapy.

C. Combined chemotherapy and radiotherapy.

D. Chemotherapy alone.

Ans. C

Q 223. The commonest cause of an obliterative stricture of the membranous urethra is:

A. Fall-astride injury.

B. Road-traffic accident with fracture pelvis and rupture urethra.

C. Prolonged catheterization.

D. Gonococcal infection

Ans. B

Q 224. Which of the following is an absolute indication for surgery in cases of benign prostatic hyperplasia?

A. Bilateral hydroureteronephrosis.

B. Nocturnal frequency.

C. Recurrent urinary tract infection.

D. Voiding bladder pressures >50 cm of water.

Ans. A

Q 225. A 27 year old man presents with a left testicular tumor with a 10 cm retroperitoneal lymph node mass. The treatment of choice is:

A. Radiotherapy.

B. Immunotherapy with interferon and inter-leukins.

C. Left high inguinal orchidectomy plus chemotherapy.

D. Chemotherapy alone.

Ans. C

Q 226. The best time for Surgery of hypospadias is:

A. 1-4 months of age.

B. 6-10 months of age.

C. 12-18 months of age.

D. 2-4 years of age.

Ans. B

Q 227. The Hunterian Ligature operation is performed for:

A. Varicose veins.

B. Arteriovenous fistulae.

C. Aneurysm.

D. Acute ischemia.

Ans. C

Q 228. Sympathectomy is indicated in all the following conditions except:

A. Ischaemic ulcers.

B. Intermittent claudication.

C. Anhidrosis.

D. Acrocyanosis.

Ans. C

Orthopaedics

Q 229. Commonest cause for neuralgic pain in foot is:

A. Compression of communication between medial and lateral plantar nerve.

B. Exaggeration of longitudinal arches.

C. Injury to deltoid ligament.

D. Shortening of plantar aponeurosis.

Ans. A

Q 230. In actinomycosis of the spine, the abscess usually erodes:

A. Intervertebral disc

B. Into the pleural cavity

C. Into the retroperitoneal space

D. Towards the SKIN

Ans. D

Q 231. A ten-year old girl presents with swelling of one knee joint. All of the following conditions can be considered in the differential diagnosis, except:

A. Tuberculosis

B. Juvenile rheumatoid arthritis

C. Haemophilia

D. Villonodular synovitis

Ans. C

Q 232. Avascular necrosis can be a possible sequelae of FRACTURE of all of the

following bones, except:

A. Femur neck

B. Scaphoid

C. Talus

D. Calcaneum

Ans. D

Q 233. Sciatic nerve palsy may occur in the following injury:

A. Posterior dislocation of hip joint.

B. FRACTURE neck of femur.

C. Trochanteric FRACTURE .

D. Anterior dislocation of hip.

Ans. A

Q 234. A 30-year old male was brought to the casualty following a road traffic accident. His physical examination revealed that his right lower limb was short, internally rotated and flexed and adducted at the hip. The most likely diagnosis is:

A. FRACTURE neck of femur.

B. Trochanteric FRACTURE .

C. Central FRACTURE dislocation of hip.

D. Posterior dislocation of hip.

Ans. D

Q 235. Which one of the following tests will you adopt while examining a knee joint where you suspect an old tear of anterior cruciate ligament?

A. Posterior drawer test.

B. McMurray test.

C. Lachman test.

D. Pivot shift test.

Ans. C

Q 236. An eight-year old boy presents with back pain and mild fever. His plain X-ray of the dorsolumbar spine reveals a solitary collapsed dorsal vertebra with preserved disc spaces. There was no associated soft tissue shadow. The most likely diagnosis is:

A. Ewings sarcoma.

B. Tuberculosis.

C. Histiocytosis.

D. Metastasis.

Ans. C

Q 237. Kienbocks disease is due to avascular necrosis of:

A. Femoral neck.

B. Medial cuneiform bone.

C. Lunate bone.

D. Scaphoid bone.

Ans. C

Q 238. Pseudoclaudication is due to compression of:

A. Femoral artery.

B. Femoral nerve.

C. Cauda Equina.

D. Popliteal artery.

Ans. C

Anaesthesia

Q 239. An anaesthetist orders a new attendent to bring the oxygen cylinder. He will ask the attendent to identify the correct cylinder by following color code:

A. Black cylinder with white shoulder.

B. Black cylinder with grey shoulder.

C. White cylinder with black shoulder.

D. Grey cylinder with white shoulder.

Ans. A

Q 240. During rapid sequence induction of Anaesthesia :

A. Sellicks maneuver is not required.

B. Pre-oxygenation is mandatory.

C. Suxamethonium is contraindicated.

D. Patient is mechanically ventilated before endotracheal intubation.

Ans. B

Q 241. A 5 year old boy suffering from Duchenne muscular dystrophy has to undergo tendon lengthening procedure. The most appropriate anaesthetic would be:

A. Induction with intravenous thiopentone and N2O & halothane for maintenance.

B. Induction with intravenous propofol and N2O & oxygen for maintenance.

C. Induction with intravenous suxamethonium and N2O & halothane for maintenance.

D. Inhalation induction with inhalation halothane and N2O & oxygen for maintenance.

Ans. B

Q 242. A 25 year old male is undergoing incision and drainage of abscess under general Anaesthesia with spontaneous respiration. The most efficient anaesthetic circuit is:

A. Mapleson A

B. Mapleson B

C. Mapleson C

D. Mapleson D

Ans. A

Q 243. In all the following conditions neuraxial blockade is absolutely contraindicated, except:

A. Patient refusal.

B. Coagulopathy.

C. Severe hypovolemia.

D. Pre-existing neurological deficits.

Ans. D

Q 244. Interscalene approach to brachial plexus block does not provide surgical Anaesthesia in the area of distribution of which of the following nerve:

A. Musculocutaneous.

B. Ulnar.

C. Radial.

D. Median.

Ans. B

Q 245. At the end of a balanced Anaesthesia technique with non-depolarizing muscle relaxant, a patient recovered spontaneously from the effect of muscle relaxant without any reversal. Which is the most probable relaxant the patient had received?

A. Pancuronium

B. Gallamine

C. Atracuronium

D. Vecuronium

Ans. C

Q 246. A 64 year old hypertensive obese female was undergoing Surgery for fracture femur under general Anaesthesia. Intra-operatively her end tidal carbon dioxide decreased to 20 from 40 mm Hg, followed by hypotension and oxygen saturation of 85%. What would be the most probable cause:

A. Fat embolism

B. Hypovolemia

C. Bronchospasm

D. Myocardial infarction

Ans. A

Q 247. One unit of fresh blood raises the Hb% concentration by:

A. 0.1 gm%

B. 1 gm%

C. 2 gm%

D. 2.2 gm%

Ans. B

Q 248. A 50 kg. man with severe metabolic acidosis has the following parameters: pH 7.05, pCO2 12 mmHg, pO2 108 mmHg, HCO3 5 mEq/L, base excess -30 mEq/L. The approximate quantity of sodium bicarbonate that he should receive in half hour is:

A. 250 mEq.

B. 350 mEq.

C. 500 mEq.

D. 750 mEq.

Ans. A

Q 249. The induction agent of choice in day care Anaesthesia is:

A. Sevoflurane.

B. Ketamine.

C. Propofol.

D. Methohexitone.

Ans. C

Q 250. A 38 year old man is posted for extraction of last molar tooth under general Anaesthesia as a day care case. He wishes to resume his work after 6 hours. Which one of the following induction agents is preferred:

A. Thiopentone sodium.

B. Ketamine.

C. Diazepam.

D. Propofol.

Ans. D

Q 251. During cardiopulmonary resuscitation, intravenous calcium gluconate is indicated under all of the following circumstances, except:

A. After 1 min. of arrest routinely.

B. Hypocalcemia.

C. Calcium channel blocker toxicity.

D. Electromechanical dissociation.

Ans. A

Q 252. Induction agent that may cause adrenal cortex suppression is:

A. Ketamine.

B. Etomidate.

C. Propofol.

D. Thiopentone.

Ans. B

Q 253. A 40 year old lady delivered a full term baby. On examination of the baby, the neonatologist noted certain urogenital abnormality. He took the following picture. The most likely diagnosis is:

A. Urogenital sinus

B. Hypertrophied clitoris

C. Miocropenis

D. Vulval hematoma

Ans. B

Q 254. A 55 year old lady presenting to out patient department (OPD) with postmenopausal bleeding for 3 months has a 1 Ã— 1 cm nodule on the anterior lip of cervix. The most appropriate investigation to be done subsequently is:

A. Pap smear

B. Punch biopsy

C. Endocervical curettage

D. Colposcopy

Ans. B

Q 255. A hemodynamically stable nulliparous patient with ectopic pregnancy has adnexal mass of 2.5 Ã— 3 cms and beta hCG titre of 1500 miu/ml. What modality of treatment is suitable for her:

A. Conservative management

B. Medical management

C. Laparoscopic Surgery

D. Laparotomy

Ans. B

Q 256. A case of gestational trophoblastic neoplasia belongs to high risk group if disease develop after:

A. Hydatidiform mole

B. Full term pregnancy

C. Spontaneous abortion

D. Ectopic pregnancy

Ans. B

PART -3

Anatomy

Q 1. False statement regarding pudendal nerve is:

A. Both sensory and motor

B. Derived from S2,3,4 spinal nerve roots

C. Leaves pelvis through the lesser sciatic foramen

D. It is the only somatic nerve to innervate the pelvic organs

Ans. C

Q 2. Wrong statement regarding the coronary artery is:

A. Left coronary artery is present in anterior interventricular groove

B. Usually 3 obtuse marginal arteries arise from left coronary artery

C. Posterior interventricular artery arises from right coronary artery

D. Left atrial artery is a branch of left coronary artery

Ans. B

Q 3. All are true statements regarding inguinal canal except:

A. Roof is formed by conjoint tendon

B. Deep inguinal ring is formed by transversus abdominis

C. Superficial inguinal ring is formed by external oblique muscle

D. Internal oblique forms anterior and posterior wall

Ans. B

Q 4. Right gastroepiploic artery is a branch of:

A. Left gastric

B. Coeliac trunk

C. Splenic

D. Gastroduodenal

Ans. D

Q 5. In FRACTURE of middle cranial fossa, absence of tears is due to lesion in the:

A. Trigeminal ganglion

B. Ciliary ganglion

C. Lesser petrosal nerve

D. Greater petrosal nerve

Ans. D

Q 6. Motor supply to diaphragm is by:

A. Thoracodorsal nerve

B. Phrenic nerve

C. Intercostal nerves

D. Sympathetic nerves

Ans. B

Q 7. All of the following are supplied by facial nerve except:

A. Lacrimal gland

B. Submandibular gland

C. Nasal glands

D. Parotid gland

Ans. D

Q 8. In left coronary artery thrombosis, area most likely to be involved is:

A. Anterior wall of right ventricle

B. Anterior wall of left ventricle

C. Anterior wall of right atrium

D. Inferior surface of right ventricle

Ans. B

Physiology

Q 9. Tidal volume is calculated by:

A. Inspiratory capacity minus the inspiratory reserve volume

B. Total lung capacity minus the residual volume

C. Functional residual capacity minus residual volume

D. Vital capacity minus expiratory reserve volumes

Ans. A

Q 10. Surfactant production in lungs starts at:

A. 28 weeks

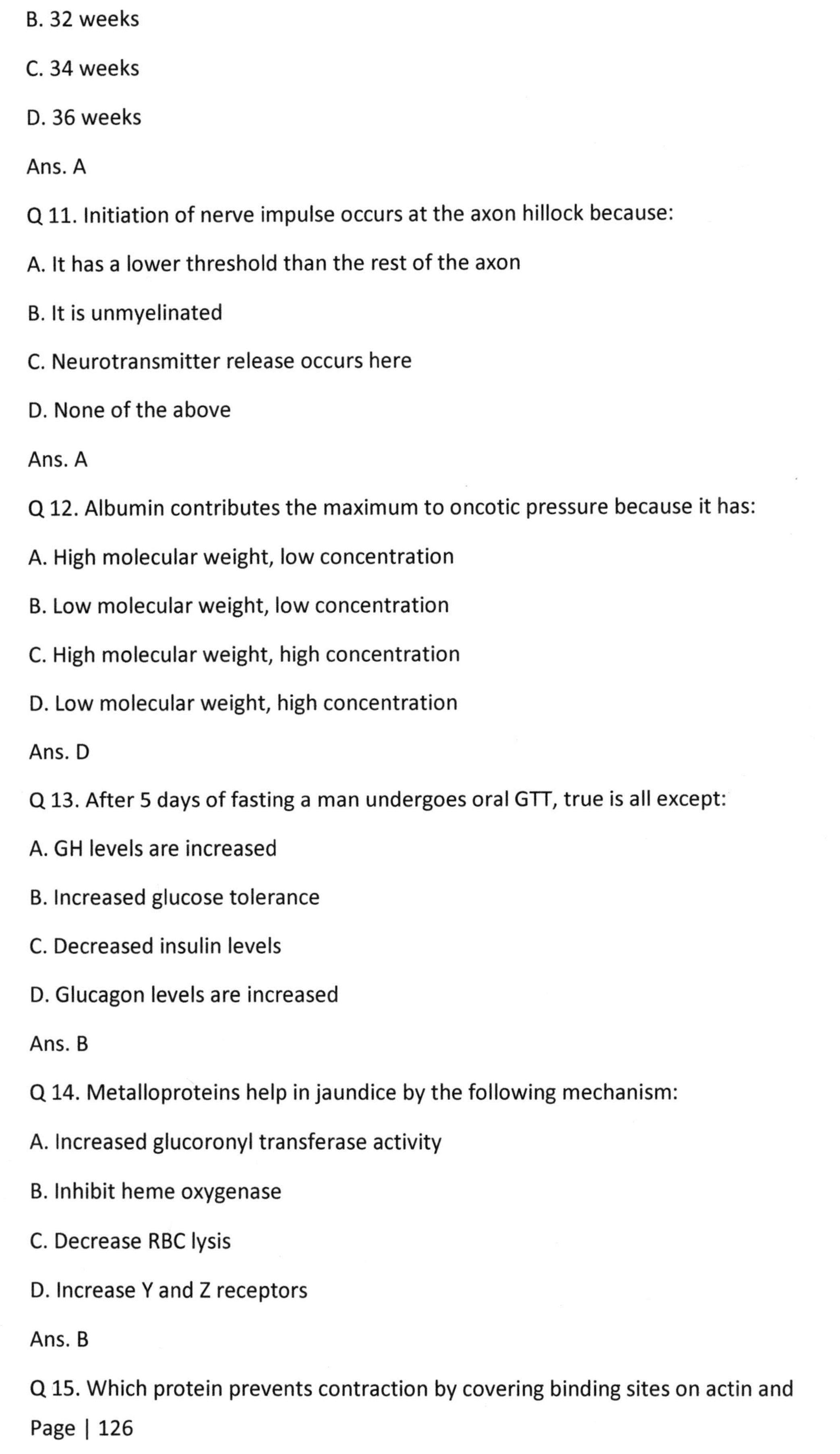

B. 32 weeks

C. 34 weeks

D. 36 weeks

Ans. A

Q 11. Initiation of nerve impulse occurs at the axon hillock because:

A. It has a lower threshold than the rest of the axon

B. It is unmyelinated

C. Neurotransmitter release occurs here

D. None of the above

Ans. A

Q 12. Albumin contributes the maximum to oncotic pressure because it has:

A. High molecular weight, low concentration

B. Low molecular weight, low concentration

C. High molecular weight, high concentration

D. Low molecular weight, high concentration

Ans. D

Q 13. After 5 days of fasting a man undergoes oral GTT, true is all except:

A. GH levels are increased

B. Increased glucose tolerance

C. Decreased insulin levels

D. Glucagon levels are increased

Ans. B

Q 14. Metalloproteins help in jaundice by the following mechanism:

A. Increased glucoronyl transferase activity

B. Inhibit heme oxygenase

C. Decrease RBC lysis

D. Increase Y and Z receptors

Ans. B

Q 15. Which protein prevents contraction by covering binding sites on actin and myosin:

A. Troponin

B. Calmodulin

C. Thymosin

D. Tropomyosin

Ans. D

Q 16. Which of the following is not correct regarding capillaries:

A. Greatest cross sectional area

B. Contain 25% of blood

C. Contains less blood than veins

D. Have single layer of cells bounding the lumen

Ans. B

Q 17. A 0.5 litre blood loss in 30 minutes will lead to:

A. Increase in HR, decrease in BP

B. Slight increase in HR, normal BP

C. Decrease in HR and BP

D. Prominent increase in HR

Ans. B

Q 18. Single most important factor in control of automatic contractility of heart is:

A. Myocardial wall thickness

B. Right atrial volume

C. SA node pacemaker potential

D. Sympathetic stimulation

Ans. D

Q 19. Which of the following is not mediated through negative FEEDBACK mechanism:

A. TSH release

B. GH formation

C. Thrombin formation

D. ACTH release

Ans. C

Q 20. Force generating proteins are:

A. Myosin and myoglobin

B. Dynein and kinesin

C. Calmodulin and G protein

D. Troponin

Ans. B

Q 21. Which is true about measurement of BP with sphygmomanometer versus intraarterial pressure measurements:

A. Less than intravascular pressure

B. More than intravascular pressure

C. Equal to intravascular pressure

D. Depends upon blood flow

Ans. B

Q 22. Secondary hyperparathyroidism due to vitamin D deficiency shows:

A. Hypocalcemia

B. Hypercalcemia

C. Hypophosphatemia

D. Hyperphosphatemia

Ans. C

Q 23. Maximum absorption of water takes place in:

A. Proximal convoluted tubule

B. Distal convoluted tubule

C. Collecting duct

D. Loop of Henle

Ans. A

Biochemistry

Q 24. Basic amino acids are:

A. Aspartate and glutamate

B. Serine and glycine

C. Lysine and arginine

D. None of the above

Ans. C

Q 25. Amino acid with dissociation constant closest to physiological pH is:

A. Serine

B. Histidine

C. Threonine

D. Proline

Ans. B

Q 26. Sources of the nitrogen in urea cycle are:

A. Aspartate and ammonia

B. glutamate and ammonia

C. Arginine and ammonia

D. Uric acid

Ans. A

Q 27. If urine sample darkens on standing: the most likely condition is:

A. Phenylketonuria

B. Alkaptonuria

C. Maple syrup disease

D. Tyrosinemia

Ans. B

Q 28. A baby presents with refusal to feed, SKIN lesions, seizures, ketosis organic acids in urine with normal ammonia; likely diagnosis is:

A. Propionic aciduria

B. Multiple carboxylase deficiency

C. Maple syrup urine disease

D. Urea cycle enzyme deficiency

Ans. B

Q 29. Force not acting in an enzyme substrate complex:

A. Electrostatic

B. Covalent

C. Van der Wall

D. Hydrogen

Ans. C

Q 30. Cellular oxidation is inhibited by:

A. Cyanide

B. Carbon dioxide

C. Chocolate

D. Carbonated beverages

Ans. A

Q 31. Triple bonds are found between which base pairs:

A. A-T

B. C-G

C. A-G

D. C-T

Ans. B

Q 32. Which of the following RNA has abnormal purine bases:

A. tRNA

B. mRNA

C. rRNA

D. 16SRNA

Ans. A

Q 33. False regarding gout is:

A. Due to increased metabolism of pyrimidines

B. Due to increased metabolism of purines

C. Uric acid levels may not be elevated

D. Has a predilection for the great toe

Ans. A

Q 34. All of the following statements are true regarding lipoproteins except:

A. VLDL transports endogenous lipids

B. LDL transports lipids to the tissues.

C. Increased blood cholesterol is associated with increased LDL receptors

D. Increased HDL is associated with decreased risk of coronary disease

Ans. C

Q 35. A destitute woman is admitted to the hospital with altered sensorium and dehydration; urine analysis shows mild proteinuria and no sugar; what other test would be desirable:

A. Fouchet

B. Rothera

C. Hays

D. Benedict

Ans. B

Q 36. Which of these fatty acids is found exclusively in breast milk?

A. Linolaete

B. Linolenic

C. Palmitic

D. d-hexanoic

Ans. A

Q 37. Blood is not a newtonian fluid because:

A. Viscosity does not changing with velocity

B. Viscosity changes with velocity

C. Density does not change with velocity

D. Density changes with velocity

Ans. B

Microbiology

Q 38. Regarding NK cells, false statement is:

A. It is activated by IL-2

B. Expresses CD 3 receptor

C. It is a variant of large lymphocyte

D. There is antibody induced proliferation of NK cells

Ans. D

Q 39. Adenosine deaminase deficiency is seen in the following:

A. Common variable immunodeficiency.

B. Severe combined immunodeficiency

C. Chronic granulomatous disease

D. Nezelof syndrome

Ans. B

Q 40. A beta hemolytic bacteria is resistant to vancomycin, shows growth in 6.5% NaCl, is non-bile sensitive. It is likely to be:

A. Strep. agalactiae

B. Strep. pneumoniae

C. Enterococcus

D. Strep. bovis

Ans. C

Q 41. False statement about the streptococcus is:

A. M protein is responsible for production of mucoid colonies

B. M protein is the major surface protein of group A streptococci

C. Mucoid colonies are virulent

D. Endotoxin causes rash of scarlet fever

Ans. A

Q 42. Toxin involved in the streptococcal toxic shock syndrome is:

A. Pyrogenic toxin

B. Erythrogenic toxin

C. Hemolysin

D. Neurotoxin

Ans. A

Q 43. A child presents with a white patch over the tonsils; diagnosis is best made by culture in:

A. Loeffler medium

B. LJ medium

C. Blood agar

D. Tellurite medium

Ans. A

Q 44. A patient with 14 days of fever is suspected of having typhoid. What investigation should be done?

A. Blood culture

B. Widal test

C. Stool culture

D. Urine culture

Ans. B

Q 45. All are true about EHEC except:

A. Sereny test is positive

B. Fails to ferment sorbitol

C. Causes HUS

D. Elaborates shiga like exotoxin

Ans. A

Q 46. An organism grown on agar shows green coloured colonies, likely organism is:

A. Staphylococcus

B. E. coli

C. Pseudomonas

D. Peptostreptococcus

Ans. C

Q 47. Congenital syphilis can be best diagnosed by:

A. IgM FTAbs

B. IgG FTAbs

C. VDRL

D. TPI

Ans. A

Q 48. All are features of Ureaplasma urealyticum except:

A. Non gonococcal urethritis

B. Salpingitis

C. Epididymitis

D. Bacterial vaginosis

Ans. D

Q 49. Regarding HIV infection, not true is:

A. p24 is used for early diagnosis

B. Lysis of infected CD 4 cells is seen

C. Dendritic cells do not support replication

D. Macrophage is a reservoir for the virus

Ans. C

Q 50. A pregnant woman from Bihar presents with hepatic encephalopathy. The likely diagnosis:

A. Hepatitis E

B. Hepatitis B

C. Sepsis

D. Acute fatty liver of pregnancy

Ans. A

Q 51. Virus causing hemorrhagic cystitis, diarrhea and conjunctivitis is:

A. RSV

B. Rhinovirus

C. Adenovirus

D. Rotavirus

Ans. C

Q 52. Cystine lactose enzyme deficient (CLED) medium is preferred over McConkey agar in UTI because:

A. Former prevents swarming of proteus

B. Is a selective medium

C. Prevents growth of pseudomonas

D. Promotes growth of candida

Ans. A

Q 53. In which stage of filariasis are microfilaria seen in peripheral blood:

A. Tropical eosinophilia

B. Early adenolymphangitis stage

C. Late adenolymphangitis stage

D. Elephantiasis

Ans. B

Q 54. Pancreatic CA is caused by:

A. Fasciola

B. Clonorchis

C. Paragonimus

D. None

Ans. B

Q 55. All of the following are true except:

A. E.coli is an aerobe and facultative anaerobe

B. Proteus forms uric acid stones

C. E. coli is motile by peritrichate flagella

D. Proteus causes deamination of phenylalanine to phenylpyruvic acid

Ans. B

Q 56. Consumption of uncooked pork is likely to cause which of the following helminthic disease:

A. Tinea saginata

B. Tinea solium

C. Hydatid cyst

D. Trichuris trichura

Ans. B

Pathology

Q 57. Enzyme that protects the brain from free radical injury is:

A. Myeloperoxidase

B. Superoxide dismutase

C. MAO

D. Hydroxylase

Ans. B

Q 58. Autoimmune haemolytic anemia is seen in:

A. ALL B. AML

C. CLL D. CML

Ans. C

Q 59. All of following are correct about thromboxane A2 except:

A. Low dose aspirin inhibits its synthesis

B. Causes vasoconstriction in blood vessels

C. Causes broncoconstriction

D. Secreted by WBC

Ans. D

Q 60. Which of the following complications is likely to result after several units of blood have been transfused?

A. Metabolic alkalosis

B. Metabolic acidosis

C. Respiratory alkalosis

D. Respiratory acidosis

Ans. A

Q 61. The mother has sickle cell disease and father is normal. Chances of children having sickle cell disease and sickle cell trait respectively are:

A. 0 and 100%

B. 25 and 25%

C. 50 and 50%

D. 10 and 50%

Ans. A

Q 62. Father has a blood group B, mother has AB; children are not likely to have the following blood group:

A. O

B. A

C. B

D. AB

Ans. A

Q 63. Protein involved in intercellular connections is:

A. Connexin

B. Integrin

C. Adhesin

D. None of the above

Ans. A

Pharmacology

Q 64. All are reasons for reducing drug dosage in elderly except:

A. They are lean and their body mass is less

B. Have decreasing renal function with age

C. Have increased baroceptor sensitivity

D. Body water is decreased

Ans. C

Q 65. True statement regarding inverse agonists is:

A. Binds to receptor and causes intended action

B. Binds to receptor and causes opposite action

C. Binds to receptor and causes no action

D. Binds to receptor and causes submaximal action

Ans. B

Q 66. True statement regarding first order kinetics is:

A. Independent of plasma concentration

B. A constant proportion of plasma concentration is eliminated

C. TÂ½ increases with dose

D. Clearance decreases with dose

Ans. B

Q 67. A diabetic female on INH and rifampicin for TB suffers DVT. She is started on warfarin. PT is not raised. Next step should be:

A. Long term heparin therapy

B. Replace warfarin with acecoumarin

C. Switch ethambutol for rifampin

D. Use LMW heparin

Ans. C

Q 68. Beta blocker that can be used in renal failure is:

A. Propranolol

B. Pindolol

C. Sotalol

D. Nadolol

Ans. A

Q 69. All of the following are correct about steroids except:

A. Inhibit the release of arachidonic acid from vessel wall through action of phospholipase A2

B. Bind plasma membrane receptors and following internalization influence nuclear changes

C. Inhibit vascular membrane permeability

D. Increase glucose synthesis, glycogen deposition in liver

Ans. B

Q 70. All of the following statements are true except:

A. PGs and leukotrienes are derived from arachidonic acid

B. COX I is an inducible enzyme

C. COX II is induced by cytokines at sites of inflammation.

D. Leukotrienes cause smooth muscle constriction

Ans. B

Q 71. Which of the following is a false statement:

A. IV noradrenaline increases systolic and diastolic BP and cause tachycardia

B. IV adrenaline increases systolic BP, no change or increase diastolic BP and causes tachycardia

C. IV isoproterenol causes increase in systolic BP, decreases diastolic BP and causes tachycardia

D. Dopamine improves renal function, increases cardiac output and systolic BP

Ans. A

Q 72. Digoxin is not indicated in:

A. Atrial flutter

B. Atrial fibrillation

C. High output failure

D. PSVT

Ans. C

Q 73. All of the following statements are true about theophylline except:

A. Increase in dose is required in cardiopulmonary disease

B. Increases cAMP

C. Increase in dose is required in smokers

D. Inhibits phosphodiesterase

Ans. A

Q 74. Mechanism of action of tetracycline is:

A. Binds to A site and inhibit attachment of t-RNA.

B. Inhibits peptidyl transferase

C. Causes misreading of mRNA

D. Causes termination of peptide chain elongation

Ans. A

Q 75. False statement about selegeline is:

A. It is a MAO-A inhibitor

B. Does not cause cheese reaction

C. Not useful in advanced cases of on-off phenomenon

D. It is used in parkinsonism

Ans. A

Q 76. A patient on phenytoin for treatment of seizures develops depression for which he is prescribed tricyclics. He now complains of lassitude and his Hb reads 8. Next step in managing this patient should be:

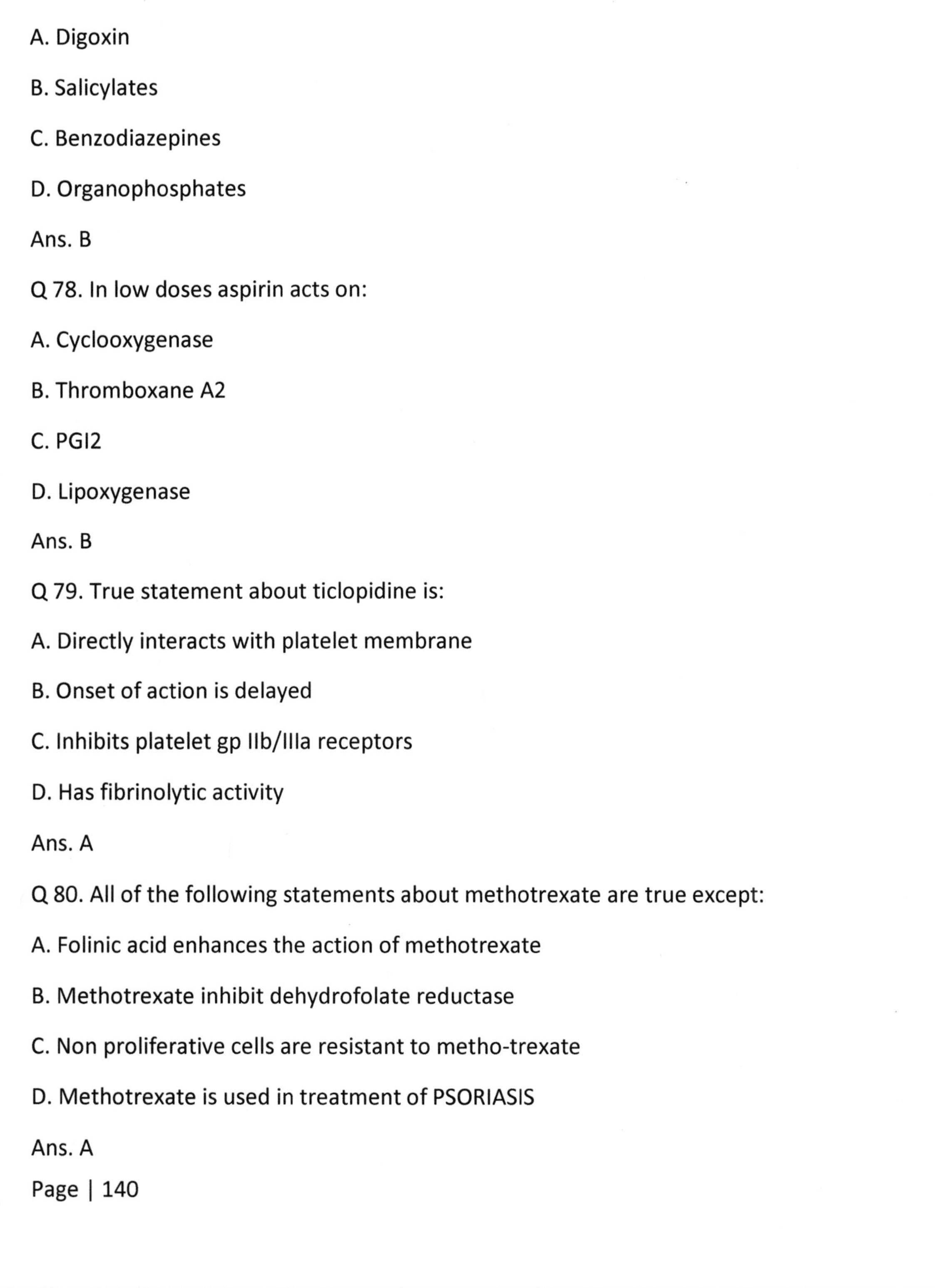

A. Chest X-ray

B. MCV should be estimated

C. GGT should be estimated

D. Bone marrow examination

Ans. B

Q 77. Which of the following drugs would be removed by dialysis?

A. Digoxin

B. Salicylates

C. Benzodiazepines

D. Organophosphates

Ans. B

Q 78. In low doses aspirin acts on:

A. Cyclooxygenase

B. Thromboxane A2

C. PGI2

D. Lipoxygenase

Ans. B

Q 79. True statement about ticlopidine is:

A. Directly interacts with platelet membrane

B. Onset of action is delayed

C. Inhibits platelet gp IIb/IIIa receptors

D. Has fibrinolytic activity

Ans. A

Q 80. All of the following statements about methotrexate are true except:

A. Folinic acid enhances the action of methotrexate

B. Methotrexate inhibit dehydrofolate reductase

C. Non proliferative cells are resistant to metho-trexate

D. Methotrexate is used in treatment of PSORIASIS

Ans. A

Q 81. Drug containing two sulfhydryl groups in a molecule:

A. BAL

B. EDTA

C. Pencillamine

D. Desferioxamine

Ans. A

Forensic Medicine

Q 82. Gettler test is done for death by:

A. Drowning B. Hanging

C. Bums D. Phophorus poisoning

Ans. A

Q 83. Feature indicative of antimortem drowning is:

A. Cutis anserina

B. Rigor mortis

C. Washer woman feet

D. Grass and weeds grasped in the hand

Ans. D

Q 84. A boy has 20 permanent teeth and 8 temporary teeth. His age is likely to be:

A. 9 years

B. 10 years

C. 11 years

D. 12 years

Ans. C

Q 85. A patient has sensation of bugs crawling all over his body. This may be effect of:

A. Cocaine

B. Alcohol

C. Cannabis

D. Benzodiazepines

Ans. A

Q 86. A person comes in contact with other. This is called:

A. Locard principle

B. Quetlet rule

C. Petty principle

D. None of the above

Ans. A

Q 87. A patient of head injury, has no relatives and requires urgent cranial decompression; Doctor should:

A. Operate without formal consent

B. Take police consent

C. Wait for relatives to take consent

D. Take magistrate consent

Ans. A

Q 88. A boy attempts suicide. He is brought to a private doctor and he is successfully cured. Doctor should:

A. Inform police

B. Not required to inform police

C. Report to magistrate

D. Refer to a psychiatrist

Ans. B

PREVENTIVE & SOCIAL MEDICINE

Q 89. All are true about DOTS except:

A. Continuation phase drugs are given in a multi-blister combipack

B. Medication is to be taken in presence of a health worker

C. Alternate day treatment

D. Improves compliance

Ans. C

Q 90. Basanti a 29 years aged female from Bihar presents with active tuberculosis. She delivers baby. All of the following are indicated except:

A. Administer INH to the baby

B. Withhold breastfeeding

C. Give ATT to mother for 2 years

D. Ask mother to ensure proper disposal of sputum

Ans. B

Q 91. Under the national TB programme, for a PHC to be called a PHC-R, requisite is:

A. Microscopy

B. Microscopy plus Radiology

C. Radiology

D. None of the above

Ans. B

Q 92. A person has received complete immunization against tetanus 10 years ago, now he presents with a clean wound without any lacerations from an injury sustained 3 hours ago. He should now be given:

A. Full course of tetanus toxoid

B. Single dose of tetanus toxoid

C. Human tetanus globulin

D. Human tetanus globulin and single dose of toxoid

Ans. B

Q 93. The false statement regarding tetanus is:

A. Five doses of immunisation provide life long immunity

B. TT affords no protection in the present injury

C. TIG is useful in lacerated wound

D. TT and Ig both may be given in suspected tetanus

Ans. A

Q 94. A certain community has 100 children out of whom 28 are immunised against measles. 2 of them acquired measles simultaneously. Subsequently 14 get measles. Assuming the efficacy of the vaccine to be 100%. What is the secondary attack rate?

A. 5%

B. 10%

C. 20%

D. 21.5%

Ans. C

Q 95. A community has a population of 10,000 and a birth rate of 36 per 1000. 5 maternal deaths were reported in the current year. The MMR is:

A. 14.5

B. 13.8

C. 20

D. 5

Ans. B

Q 96. 10 babies are born in a hospital on same day. All weigh 2.8 kg each. Calculate the standard deviation:

A. Zero

B. One

C. Minus one

D. 0.28

Ans. A

Q 97. Out of 11 births in a hospital, 5 babies weighed over 2.5 kg and 5 weighed less than 2.5 kg. What value does 2.5 represent:

A. Geometric average

B. Arithmetic average

C. Median

D. Mode

Ans. C

Q 98. A man weighing 68 kg, consumes 325 gm carbohydrate, 65 gm protein and 35 gms fat in his diet. The most applicable statement here is:

A. His total calorie intake is 3000 kcal

B. The proportion of proteins, fats and carbohydrates is correct and in accordance with a balanced diet

C. He has a negative nitrogen balance

D. 30% of his total energy intake is derived from fat

Ans. B

Q 99. A country has a population of 1000 million; birth rate is 23 and death rate is 6. In which phase of the demographic cycle does this country lie:

A. Early expanding

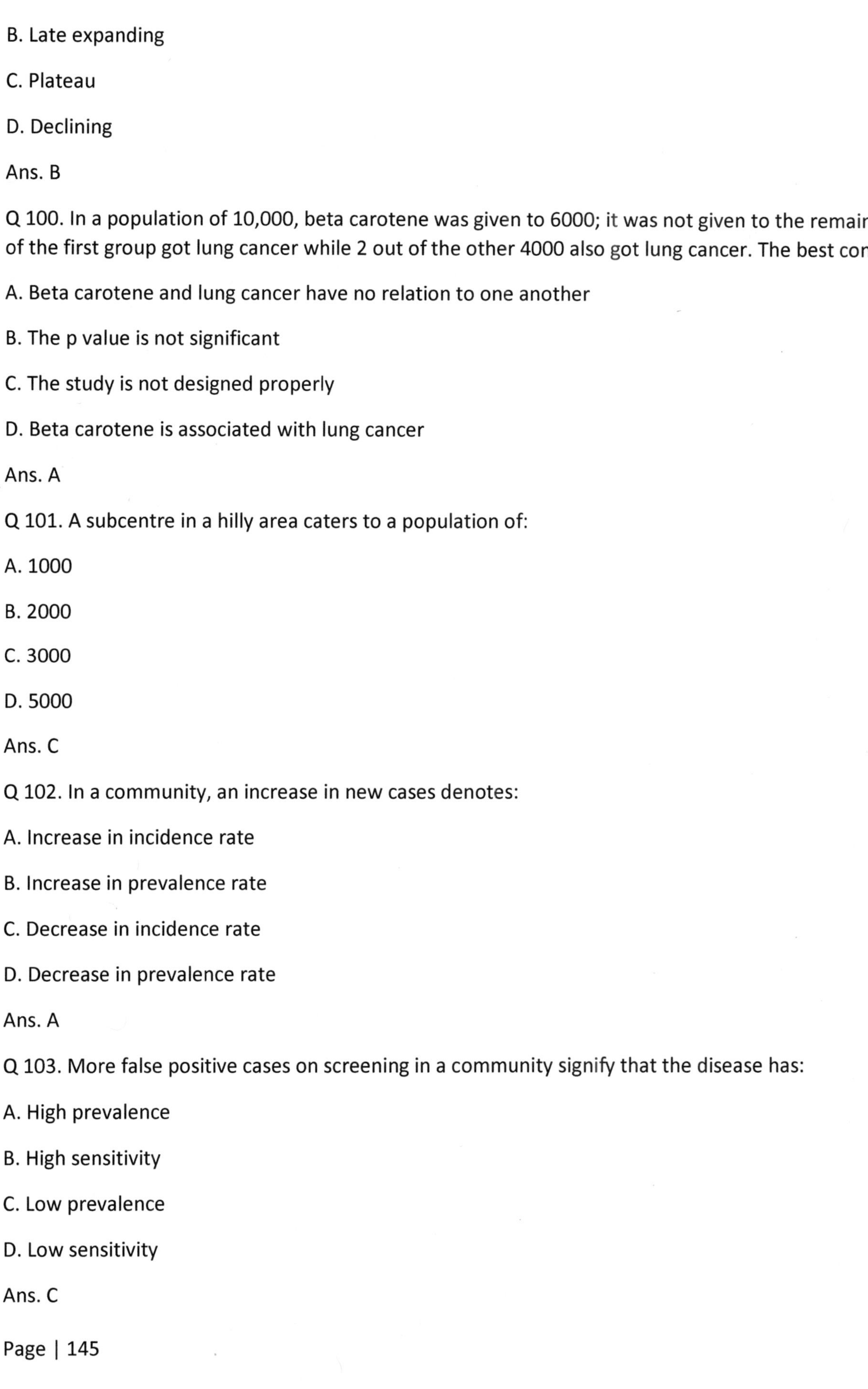

B. Late expanding

C. Plateau

D. Declining

Ans. B

Q 100. In a population of 10,000, beta carotene was given to 6000; it was not given to the remainder. 3 out of the first group got lung cancer while 2 out of the other 4000 also got lung cancer. The best conclusion is:

A. Beta carotene and lung cancer have no relation to one another

B. The p value is not significant

C. The study is not designed properly

D. Beta carotene is associated with lung cancer

Ans. A

Q 101. A subcentre in a hilly area caters to a population of:

A. 1000

B. 2000

C. 3000

D. 5000

Ans. C

Q 102. In a community, an increase in new cases denotes:

A. Increase in incidence rate

B. Increase in prevalence rate

C. Decrease in incidence rate

D. Decrease in prevalence rate

Ans. A

Q 103. More false positive cases on screening in a community signify that the disease has:

A. High prevalence

B. High sensitivity

C. Low prevalence

D. Low sensitivity

Ans. C

Q 104. The same screening test is applied to two communities X and Y; Y shows more false +ve cases as compared to X. The possibility is:

A. High sensitivity

B. High specificity

C. Y community has high prevalence

D. Y community has low prevalence

Ans. C

Q 105. ELISA is performed on a population with low prevalence of hepatitis B. What would be the result of performing double screening ELISA tests?

A. Increased sensitivity and positive predictive value

B. Increased sensitivity and negative predictive value

C. Increased specificity and positive predictive value

D. Increased specificity and negative predictive value

Ans. C

Q 106. While testing a hypolipidemic drug, serum lipid levels were tested both before and after its use. Which test is best suited for the statistical analysis of the result:

A. Paired t-test

B. Student test

C. Chi square test

D. None of the above

Ans. A

Q 107. Type 1 sampling error is classified as:

A. Alpha error

B. Beta error

C. Gamma error

D. Delta error

Ans. A

Q 108. Virulence of a disease is indicated by:

A. Proportional mortality rate

B. Specific mortality rate

C. Case fatality ratio

D. Amount of GDP spent on control of disease

Ans. C

Q 109. Which of the following diseases needs not to be screened for in workers to be employed in a dye industry in Gujarat?

A. Anemia

B. Bronchial asthma

C. Bladder cancer

D. Precancerous lesion

Ans. A

Q 110. Best test to detect iron deficiency in community is:

A. Serum transferrin

B. Serum ferritin

C. Serum iron

D. Hemoglobin

Ans. B

Q 111. Which of the following is not a complete sterilization agent?

A. Glutaraldehyde

B. Absolute alcohol

C. Hydrogen peroxide

D. Sodium hypochlorite

Ans. B

Q 112. Seasonal trend is due to:

A. Vector variation

B. Environmental factors

C. Change in herd immunity

D. All of the above

Ans. B

Medicine

Q 113. False statement about type I respiratory failure is:

A. Decreased PaO2

B. Decreased PaCO2

C. Normal PaCO2

D. Normal A-a gradient

Ans. D

Q 114. A 60 years old man presents with nonproductive cough for 4 weeks. He has grade III clubbing, and a lesion in the apical lobe on X-ray. Most likely diagnosis here is:

A. Small cell CA

B. Non-small cell CA

C. Fungal infection

D. Tuberculosis

Ans. B

Q 115. A 60 years old man is suspected of having bronchogenic CA. TB has been ruled out in this patient. What should be the next investigation?

A. CT guided FNAC

B. Bronchoscopy and biopsy

C. Sputum cytology

D. X-ray chest

Ans. B

Q 116. A man presents with fever, weight loss and cough. Mantoux reads an induration of 17 Ã— 19 mm; sputum cytology is negative for AFB. Most likely diagnosis is:

A. Pulmonary tuberculosis

B. Fungal infection

C. Viral infection

D. Pneumonia

Ans. A

Q 117. Pulmonary edema associated with normal PCWP is observed, which of these is not a cause:

A. High altitude

B. Cocaine overdose

C. Post cardiopulmonary bypass

D. Bilateral renal artery stenosis

Ans. D

Q 118. An ABG analysis shows: pH 7.2, raised pCO2, decreased HCO3. Diagnosis is:

A. Respiratory acidosis

B. Compensated metabolic acidosis

C. Respiratory and metabolic acidosis

D. Respiratory alkalosis

Ans. C

Q 119. ABG analysis of a patient on ventilator shows decreased pCO2, normal pO2, pH 7.5. Diagnosis is:

A. Respiratory acidosis

B. Metabolic alkalosis

C. Respiratory alkalosis

D. Metabolic acidosis

Ans. C

Q 120. In a patient of acute inferior wall MI. Best modality of treatment is:

A. IV fluids

B. Digoxin

C. Diuretics

D. Vasodilators

Ans. A

Q 121. A 26 years old asymptomatic woman is found to have arrhythmias and a systolic murmur associated with midsystolic. Which investigation would you use?

A. Electrophysiological testing

B. CT scan

C. Echocardiography

D. Angiography

Ans. C

Q 122. A patient complains of intermittent claudication, dizziness and headache. Most likely cardiac lesion is:

A. TOF

B. ASD

C. PDA

D. Coarctation of aorta

Ans. D

Q 123. All of the following are true about ASD except:

A. Right atrial hypertrophy

B. Left atrial hypertrophy

C. Right ventricular hypertrophy

D. Pulmonary hypertension

Ans. B

Q 124. Mitral valve vegetations do not usually embolise to:

A. Lung

B. liver

C. spleen

D. brain

Ans. A

Q 125. A woman has septic abortion done, vegetation on tricuspid valve is likely to go to:

A. Septic infarcts to lung

B. liver

C. spleen infarcts

D. Emboli to brain

Ans. A

Q 126. Kussmaul sign is not seen in:

A. Restrictive cardiomyopathy

B. Constrictive pericarditis

C. Cardiac tamponade

D. RV infarct

Ans. C

Q 127. A patient presents with engorged neck veins, BP 80/50 mmHg and pulse rate of 100/min following blunt trauma to the chest. Diagnosis is:

A. Pneumothorax

B. Right ventricular failure

C. Cardiac tamponade

D. Hemothorax

Ans. C

Q 128. Which of the following is not seen on hemoglobin electrophoresis in sickle cell anemia?

A. HbA

B. HbA2

C. HbF

D. HbS

Ans. A

Q 129. False statement regarding DIC is:

A. Thrombocytopenia

B. Decreased fibrinogen

C. Decreased PTT

D. Increased PT

Ans. C

Q 130. Thrombocytopenia occurs in all except:

A. Henoch Schonlein purpura

B. TTP

C. DIC

D. Leukemia

Ans. A

Q 131. A patient with an Hb of 6 g%, WBC count of 2000/cmm, has a normal different count except for having 6% blasts, platelets are reduced to 80,000/cmm; moderate splenomegaly is present. Possible diagnosis is:

A. Leukemia

B. Aplastic anemia

C. HEMOLYSIS

D. ITP

Ans. A

Q 132. A patient being investigated for anemia has a dry marrow tap; peripheral smear reveals tear drop cells. Most likely diagnosis is:

A. Leukemia

B. Lymphoma

C. Myelofibrosis

D. Polycythemia rubra vera

Ans. C

Q 133. Tumor associated with polycythemia vera is:

A. Sarcoma

B. Pituitary adenoma

C. Cerebellar haemangioblastoma

D. None of the above

Ans. C

Q 134. A young patient presents with jaundice. Total bilirubin is 21 mg%, direct is 9.6 mg%, alkaline phosphatase is 84 KA units. Diagnosis is:

A. Hemolytic jaundice

B. Viral hepatitis

C. Chronic active hepatitis

D. Obstructive jaundice

Ans. D

Q 135. A young male with gallbladder stones shows the following test results:

serum bilirubin 2.5 mg%, Hb 6 g%, urine test positive for urobilinogen. Diagnosis is:

A. Hemolytic jaundice

B. Obstructive jaundice

C. Hepatocellular jaundice

D. Protoporphyria

Ans. A

Q 136. An 18 years old male presents with massive hematemesis. He has history of fever for the past 14 days for which he was managed with drugs. Moderate splenomegaly is present. Diagnosis is:

A. NSAID induced duodenal ulcer

B. Drug induced gastritis

C. Esophageal varices

D. None of the above

Ans. C

Q 137. Urinalysis shows RBC casts. Likely source is:

A. kidney

B. Ureter

C. Bladder

D. Urethra

Ans. A

Q 138. A young man develops gross hematuria 3 days after an attack of URTI. Most likely renal Pathology is:

A. Acute glomerulonephritis

B. Minimal change disease

C. IgA nephropathy

D. Membranous glomerulonephritis

Ans. C

Q 139. A patient CSF report reads as follows: sugar 40 mg%, protein 150 mg%, chloride 550 mg%; lymphocytosis present. The picture is suggestive of:

A. Fungal meningitis

B. Viral meningitis

C. TB meningitis

D. Leukemia

Ans. C

Q 140. Lacunar infarcts are caused by:

A. Lipohyalinosis of penetrating arteries

B. Middle carotid artery involvement

C. Emboli to anterior circulation

D. None of the above

Ans. A

Q 141. Dinesh, a 56 years aged man presents with complaints of slowness of movements, postural instability, tremors, rigidity and memory loss. Most likely diagnosis is:

A. Multi-infarct dementia

B. Alzheimer disease

C. Parkinsonism

D. None of the above

Ans. C

Q 142. All of the following may be seen in Wilson disease except:

A. Cerebellar ataxia

B. Peripheral neuropathy

C. Dysphagia

D. Chorea

Ans. B

Q 143. An elderly man presents with features of dementia, ataxia, difficulty in downward gaze and a history of frequent falls. Likely diagnosis is:

A. Parkinson disease

B. Progressive supranuclear gaze palsy

C. Alzheimer disease

D. None of the above.

Ans. B

Q 144. A chromosomal anomaly associated with Alzheimer dementia is:

A. Trisomy 18

B. Patau syndrome

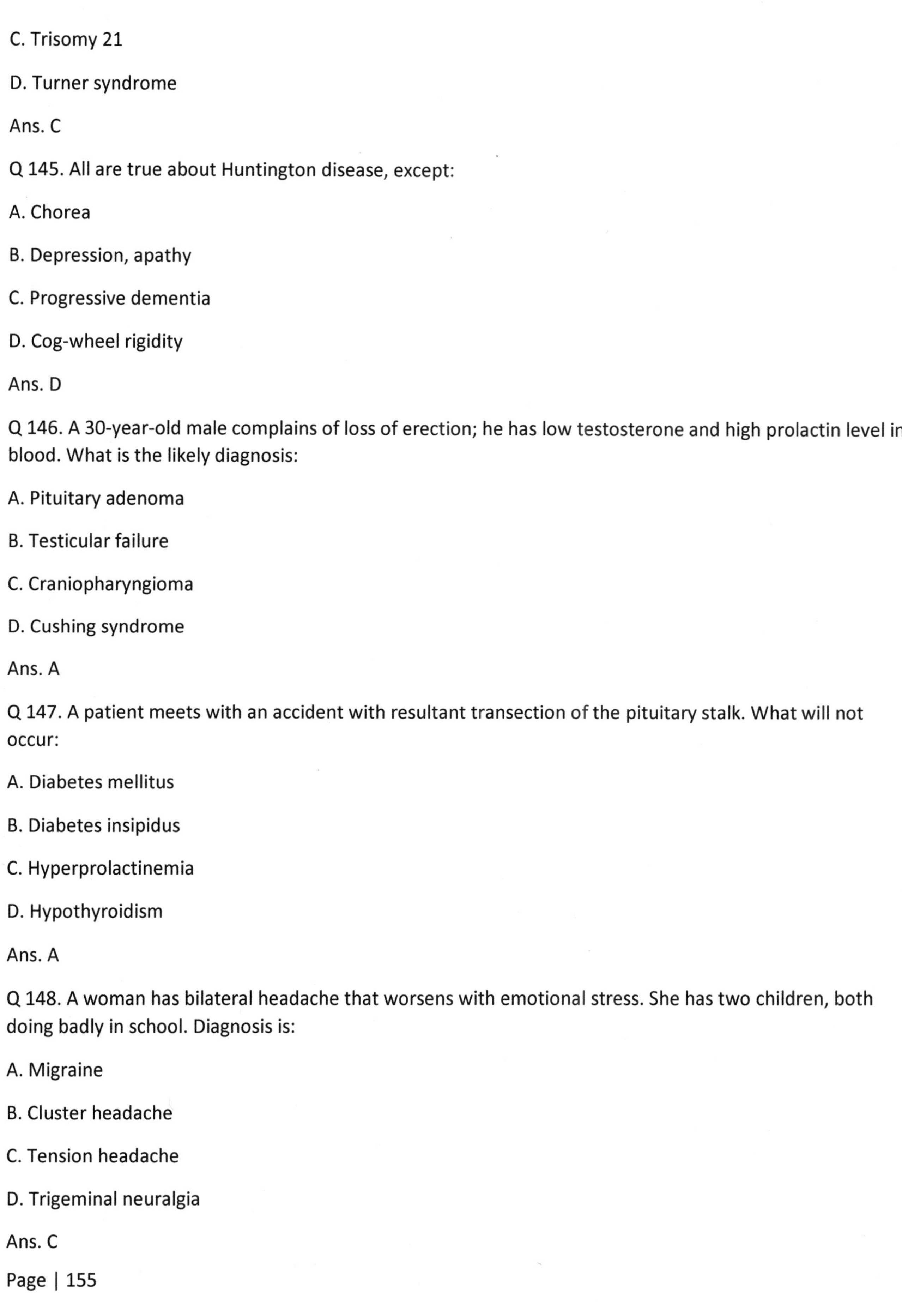

C. Trisomy 21

D. Turner syndrome

Ans. C

Q 145. All are true about Huntington disease, except:

A. Chorea

B. Depression, apathy

C. Progressive dementia

D. Cog-wheel rigidity

Ans. D

Q 146. A 30-year-old male complains of loss of erection; he has low testosterone and high prolactin level in blood. What is the likely diagnosis:

A. Pituitary adenoma

B. Testicular failure

C. Craniopharyngioma

D. Cushing syndrome

Ans. A

Q 147. A patient meets with an accident with resultant transection of the pituitary stalk. What will not occur:

A. Diabetes mellitus

B. Diabetes insipidus

C. Hyperprolactinemia

D. Hypothyroidism

Ans. A

Q 148. A woman has bilateral headache that worsens with emotional stress. She has two children, both doing badly in school. Diagnosis is:

A. Migraine

B. Cluster headache

C. Tension headache

D. Trigeminal neuralgia

Ans. C

Q 149. A female aged 30 years, presents with episodic throbbing headache for past 4 years with nausea and vomiting. Most likely diagnosis is:

A. Migraine

B. Cluster headache

C. Angle closure glaucoma

D. Temporal arteritis

Ans. A

Q 150. A woman complains of headache associated with paresthesias of the right upper and lower limb. Most likely diagnosis is:

A. Trigeminal neuralgia

B. Glossopharyngeal neuralgia

C. Migraine

D. Cluster headache

Ans. C

Q 151. All of the following are features of MEN IIa, except:

A. Pituitary tumor

B. Pheochromocytoma

C. Medullary CA thyroid

D. Parathyroid adenoma

Ans. A

Q 152. A patient with Cushingoid features presents with hemoptysis. He shows no response to dexamethasone suppression test. Most likely diagnosis is:

A. Adrenal hyperplasia

B. Adrenal adenoma

C. CA lung with ectopic ACTH production

D. Pituitary microadenoma

Ans. C

Q 153. An obese patient presented in casualty in an unconscious state. His blood sugar measured 400 mg%, urine tested positive for sugar and ketones. Drug most useful in management is:

A. Glibenclamide

B. Troglitazone

C. Insulin

D. Chlorpropamide

Ans. C

Q 154. Which of the following is not associated with thymoma?

A. Red cell aplasia

B. Myasthenia gravis

C. Hypergammaglobulinemia

D. Compression of the superior mediastinum

Ans. C

Q 155. A young basketball player with height 188 cm and arm span 197 cm has a diastolic murmur best heard in second right intercostal space. Likely cause of murmur is:

A. AS

B. Coarctation of aorta

C. AR

D. MR

Ans. C

Q 156. A patient presents with arthritis, hyperpigmen-tation of SKIN and hypogonadism. Likely diagnosis is:

A. Hemochromatosis

B. Ectopic ACTH secreting tumor of lung

C. Wilson disease

D. Rheumatoid arthrits

Ans. A

Q 157. In myasthenia gravis, correct statement regarding thymectomy is:

A. Should be done in all cases

B. Should be done in cases with ocular involvement only

C. Not required if controlled by medical management

D. Should be done only in cases that are associated with thymoma

Ans. A

Q 158. Most common fungal infection in febrile neutropenia is:

A. Aspergillus niger

B. Candida

C. Mucormycosis

D. Aspergillus fumigatus

Ans. B

Q 159. The following group of tests should be done to optimise graft uptake in bone marrow transplant:

A. Blood grouping

B. HLA matching

C. Culture for infection

D. All of the above

Ans. B

Q 160. True statement about neurocysticercosis is:

A. Seizures due to neurocysticercosis are resistant to antiepileptic drugs

B. Albendazole is superior to praziquantel in the treatment of above condition

C. Common presentation is 6th cranial nerve palsy and hemiparesis

D. Steroids are used in the management of hydrocephalus

Ans. B

Q 161. All of the following are true regarding a patient with acid peptic disease except:

A. Misoprostol is the drug of choice in patients on NSAIDs

B. DU is preventable by the use of single night-time H2 blockers

C. Omeprazole may help ulcers refractory to H2 blockers

D. Misoprostol is DOC in pregnant patients

Ans. D

Q 162. A man presents with mass at duodenojejunal flexure invading renal papillae. Histopathology reports it as lymphoma. True statement is:

A. II E stage

B. III E stage

C. IV E stage

D. Staging cannot be done until bone marrow examination is performed

Ans. C

Q 163. A 45 years male presents with hypertension. He has sudden abnormal flinging movements in right upper and lower limbs. Most likely site of hemorrahge is:

A. Substantia nigra

B. Caudate nuclei

C. Pons

D. Subthalamic nuclei

Ans. D

Q 164. True about haemophilia A are all except:

A. PTT increased

B. PT increased

C. Clotting time is increased

D. Serum levels of factor VIII are decreased

Ans. B

Q 165. IPPV can cause:

A. Barotrauma

B. Pleural effusion

C. Increased venous return

D. None of the above

Ans. A

Q 166. Characteristic finding in CT in a TB is:

A. Exudate seen in basal cistern

B. Hydrocephalus is non communicating

C. Calcification commonly seen in cerebellum

D. Ventriculitis is a common finding

Ans. A

Q 167. Vegetations on undersurface of AV valves are found in:

A. Acute rheumatic carditis

B. Limban Sack endocarditis

C. Non thrombotic bacterial endocarditis

D. Chronic rheumatic carditis

Ans. B

Q 168. Triage means:

A. Sorting out of cases on availability of medical resources and severity of patient condition

B. Patients are divided into 3 groups

C. Severely injured patients are attended first in military camps

D. None of the above

Ans. A

PEDIATRICS

Q 169. Which of the following is not true about atrial septal defect?

A. There is a defect in region of fossa ovalis

B. Blood flow from left atrium to right atrium

C. Increased blood flow through lungs lead to pulmonary plethora

D. There is splitting of first heart sound

Ans. D

Q 170. A neonate presents with jaundice and clay white stools. On liver biopsy giant cells are seen. Most likely diagnosis is:

A. Physiological jaundice

B. Neonatal hepatitis with extra biliary atresia

C. Neonatal hepatitis with physiological jaundice

D. Extra biliary atresia

Ans. B

Q 171. A newborn has dribbling after feeds. He has respiratory distress and froth at the mouth. Diagnosis is:

A. Tracheoesophageal fistula

B. Tetralogy of Fallot

C. Respiratory distress syndrome

D. None of the above

Ans. A

Q 172. Ramu, a 8-years-old boy presents with upper GI bleeding. On examination, he is found to have splenomegaly; there are no signs of ascites, or hepatomegaly; esophageal varices are found on UGIE. Most likely diagnosis is:

A. Budd Chiari syndrome

B. Non cirrhotic portal fibrosis

C. Cirrhosis

D. Veno-occlusive disease

Ans. B

Q 173. A 5-years-old child suffering from nephrotic syndrome is responding well to steroid therapy. What would be the most likely finding on light microscopy?

A. No finding

B. Basement membrane thickening

C. Hypercellular glomeruli

D. Fusion of foot processes

Ans. A

Q 174. Most common cause of urinary obstruction in a male infant is:

A. Anterior urethral valves

B. Posterior urethral valves

C. Stone

D. Stricture

Ans. B

Q 175. A 5-years-old child presents with a calculus of size 2 cm in the upper ureter. He also complains of haematuria. USG shows no further obstruction in the urinary tract. Treatment of choice for this patient would be:

A. Ureterolithotomy

B. Endoscopic removal

C. ESWL

D. Observation

Ans. C

Q 176. A patient presents with LVH and pulmonary complications. ECG shows left axis deviation. Most likely diagnosis is:

A. TOF

B. Tricuspid atresia

C. TAPVC

D. VSD

Ans. B

Q 177. Potts shunt is anastomosis of:

A. Right subclavian artery to right pulmonary artery

B. Descending aorta to left pulmonary artery

C. Left subclavian to left pulmonary artery

D. Ascending aorta to right pulmonary artery

Ans. B

Q 178. A neonate has recurrent attacks of abdominal pain, restless, irritability and diaphoresis on feeding. Cardiac auscultation reveals a nonspecific murmur. He is believed to be at risk for MI. Likely diagnosis is:

A. ASD

B. VSD

C. TOF

D. Anomalous coronary artery

Ans. D

Q 179. A child aged 2 years presents with nonspecific symptoms suggestive of anemia. On peripheral blood smear target cells are seen. He has hypochromic microcytic picture and Hb of 6 gm%. He also has â€˜a positive family historyâ€™. Next investigation of choice is:

A. Hb electrophoresis

B. Coombs test

C. liver function tests

D. Osmotic fragility test

Ans. A

Q 180. Most common cause of meningitis in children between 6 months to 2 years of age is:

A. Pneumococcus

B. Staphylococcus

C. H. influenzae

D. E. coli

Ans. C

Q 181. A child presents with seborrheic dermatitis, lytic skull lesions, ear discharge and hepatosplenomegaly. Likely diagnosis is:

A. Leukemia

B. Lymphoma

C. Histiocytosis X

D. Multiple myeloma

Ans. C

Q 182. Which of the following is true regarding cretinism?

A. Short limbs compared to trunk

B. Proportionate shortening

C. Short limbs and short stature

D. Short limbs and long stature

Ans. C

Q 183. Manifestations of endemic cretinism include:

A. Deafness and facial nerve involvement

B. Blindness and hypothyroidism

C. Goitre and hypothyroidism

D. Multinodular goitre and mental retardation

Ans. A

Q 184. A 10 day old male pseudohermaphrodite child with 46 XY karyotype presents with BP of 110/80 mmHg. Most likely enzyme deficiency is:

A. 21 hydroxylase

B. 17 hydroxylase

C. 11 hydroxylase

D. 3-beta hydroxylase

Ans. B

Q 185. Treatment of Kawasaki disease in children is:

A. Oral steroids

B. IV steroids

C. IV Ig

D. Mycophenolate mefentil

Ans. C

Q 186. A neonate delivered at 32 weeks, is put on a ventilator. X-ray shows â€˜white out lung and ABG reveals PO2 of 75. Ventilator settings are on, FIO2 of 70, and rate of 50/minute. Next step to be taken should be:

A. Increase rate to 60 per minute

B. Increase FIO2 to 80

C. Continue ventilation with the same settings

D. Weaning ventilator

Ans. C

Dermatology

Q 187. A man aged 50 years presents with, alopecia, boggy scalp swelling and easily pluckable hair. Next step in establishing the diagnosis would be:

A. KOH smear

B. Culture sensitivity

C. Biopsy

D. None of the above

Ans. A

Q 188. Most common organism causing tinea capitis is:

A. Trichophyton tonsurans

B. Microsporum

C. Epidermophyton

D. Candida albicans

Ans. A

Q 189. A young man aged 19 years develops a painless penile ulcer 9 days after sexual intercourse with a professional sex worker. Most likely diagnosis is:

A. Chancroid

B. Herpes

C. Primary chancre

D. Traumatic ulcer

Ans. C

Q 190. An infant presents with itchy lesions over the groin and prepuce. All of the following are indicated in this patient except:

A. Bathe and apply scabicidal solution

B. Treatment should be extended to all family members

C. Dispose all clothes by burning

D. Start the patient on IV antibiotics

Ans. D

Q 191. A boy aged 8 years from Tamil Nadu presents with a white, non anesthetic, nonscaly, hypopigmented macule on his face. Most likely diagnosis is:

A. Pityriasis alba

B. Pityriasis versicolor

C. Indeterminate leprosy

D. Pure neuritic leprosy

Ans. C

Q 192. A 20 years old, male patient, from jaipur presents with an erythematous lesion on the cheek with central crusting. Most likely diagnosis is:

A. SLE

B. LUPUS vulgaris

C. Chillblains

D. Cutaneous leishmaniasis

Ans. D

Q 193. A 19 year old pregnant girl presents with light brown pigmentation over the malar eminences. Most likely diagnosis is:

A. Chloasma

B. SLE

C. Melasma

D. Melanoma

Ans. A

Q 194. A girl aged 19, presents with arthritis and a photosensitive rash on the cheek. Likely diagnosis is:

A. SLE

B. Chloasma

C. Stevens Johnson syndrome

D. Lyme disease

Ans. A

Psychiatry

Q 195. A patient with pneumonia for 5 days is admitted to the hospital. He suddenly ceases to recognize the doctor and staff, thinks that he is in jail and complains of scorpions attacking him. He is in altered sensorium. This condition is:

A. Acute delirium

B. Acute dementia

C. Acute schizophrenia

D. Acute paranoia

Ans. A

Q 196. A person missing from home, is found wandering purposefully. He is well groomed, and denies of having any amnesia. Most likely diagnosis is:

A. Dissociative fugue

B. Dissociative amnesia

C. Schizophrenia

D. Dementia

Ans. A

Q 197. Babu, a 40 years aged male complains of sudden onset palpitations and apprehension. He is sweating for the last 10 minutes and fears of impending death. Diagnosis is:

A. Hysteria

B. Cystic fibrosis

C. Panic attack

D. Generalized anxiety disorder

Ans. C

Q 198. A lady, while driving a car meets with an accident. She was admitted in an ICU for 6 months. After being discharged, she often gets up in night and feels terrified She is afraid to sit in a car again. The diagnosis is:

A. Panic disorder

B. Phobia

C. Conversion disorder

D. Post traumatic stress disorder

Ans. D

Q 199. A patient present with waxy flexibility, negativitism and rigidity. Diagnosis is:

A. Catatonic schizophrenia

B. Paranoid schizophrenia

C. Hebephrenic schizophrenia

D. Simple schizophrenia

Ans. A

Q 200. Chandu, age 32 presents with abdominal pain and vomiting. He also complains of some psychiatric symptoms and visual hallucinations. Most likely diagnosis is:

A. Intermittent porphyria

B. Hypothyroidism

C. Hyperthyroidism

D. Hysteria

Ans. A

Q 201. Basanti 27 years aged, female thinks her nose is ugly; her idea is fixed and not shared by anyone else. Whenever she goes out of home, she hides her face with a cloth. She visits a Surgeon. Next step would be:

A. Investigate and then operate

B. Refer to psychiatrist

C. Reassure the patient

D. Immediate operation

Ans. B

Surgery

Q 202. A male aged 60 years has foul breath. He regurgitates food that is eaten 3 days ago. Likely diagnosis is:

A. Zenker diverticulum

B. Meckel diverticulum

C. Scleroderma

D. Achalasia cardia

Ans. A

Q 203. Most common site for squamous cell carcinoma esophagus is:

A. Upper third

B. Middle third

C. Lower third

D. Gastro-esophageal junction.

Ans. B

Q 204. What is true regarding congenital hypertrophic pyloric stenosis?

A. More common in girls

B. Hypochloremic alkalosis

C. Heller myotomy is the procedure of choice.

D. Most often manifests at birth

Ans. B

Q 205. Patient presents with recurrent duodenal ulcer of 2.5 cm size. Procedure of choice is:

A. Truncal vagotomy and antrectomy

B. Truncal vagotomy and gastrojejunostomy

C. Highly selective vagotomy

D. Laparoscopic vagotomy and gastrojejunostomy

Ans. A

Q 206. All are features of hyperplastic tuberculosis of gastrointestinal tract except:

A. Presents with a mass in RIF

B. Barium meal shows pulled up caecum

C. Most common site is ileocecal junction

D. ATT is the treatment of choice

Ans. D

Q 207. A 56 year old woman has not passed stools for the last 14 days. X-ray shows no air/fluid levels. Probable diagnosis is:

A. Paralytic ileus

B. Aganglionosis of the colon

C. Intestinal pseudo-obstruction

D. Duodenal obstruction.

Ans. C

Q 208. A man aged 60 years has history of IHD and atherosclerosis. He presents with abdominal pain and maroon stools. Most likely diagnosis is:

A. Acute intestinal obstruction

B. Acute mesenteric ischemia

C. Peritonitis

D. Appendicitis

Ans. B

Q 209. True statement regarding â€˜fistula in ano is:

A. Posterior fistulae have straight tracks

B. High fistulae can be operated with no fear of incontinence

C. High and low divisions are made in relation to the pelvic floor

D. Intersphincteric is the most common type

Ans. D

Q 210. In a 27 year old male most common cause of a colovesical fistula would be:

A. Crohn disease

B. Ulcerative colitis

C. TB

D. Cancer colon

Ans. A

Q 211. Following trauma, a patient presents with a drop of blood at the tip of urinary meatus. He complains of inability to pass urine. Next step should be:

A. IVP should be done

B. MCU should be done

C. Catheterize, drain bladder and remove the catheter thereafter

D. Catheterize, drain bladder and retain the catheter thereafter

Ans. D

Q 212. Chandu, a 45 years male shows calcification on the right side of his abdomen in an AP view. In lateral view the calcification is seen to overlie the spine. Most likely diagnosis is:

A. Gallstones

B. Calcified mesenteric nodes

C. Renal stones

D. Calcified rib

Ans. C

Q 213. CA prostate commonly metastasises to the vertebrae because:

A. Valveless communication exist with Batson prevertebral plexus

B. Via drainage to sacral lymph node

C. Of direct spread

D. None of above

Ans. A

Q 214. Following sexual intercourse, a person develops pain in the left testes that does not get relieved on elevation of scrotum. Diagnosis is:

A. Epididymo-orchitis

B. Torsion testis

C. Fournier gangrene

D. Tumor testes

Ans. B

Q 215. A testicular tumor in a man aged 60 years is most likely to be:

A. Germ cell tumor

B. Sertoli cell tumor

C. Teratocarcinoma

D. Lymphoma

Ans. D

Q 216. A patient presents with bilateral proptosis, heat intolerance and palpitations. Most unlikely diagnosis here would be:

A. Hashimoto thyroiditis

B. Thyroid adenoma

C. Diffuse thyroid igoitre

D. Reidel thyroiditis

Ans. D

Q 217. A patient with long standing multinodular goitre develops hoarseness of voice. Also, the swelling undergoes sudden increase in size. Likely diagnosis is:

A. Follicular CA

B. Papillary CA

C. Medullary CA

D. Anaplastic CA

Ans. A

Q 218. A patient presents with swelling in the neck following a thyroidectomy. What is the most likely resulting complication?

A. Respiratory obstruction

B. Recurrent laryngeal nerve palsy

C. Hypovolemia

D. Hypocalcemia

Ans. A

Q 219. A patient on the same evening following thyroidectomy presents with a swelling in the neck and difficulty in breathing. Next management would be:

A. Open sutures immediately

B. Intubate oro-tracheally

C. Wait and watch

D. Administer oxygen by mask

Ans. A

Q 220. Patient presents with neck swelling and respiratory distress few hours after a thyroidectomy Surgery. Next management would be:

A. Open immediately

B. Tracheostomy

C. Wait and watch

D. Oxygen by mask

Ans. A

Q 221. A patient undergoes thyroid Surgery , following which he develops perioral tingling. Blood Ca2+ is 8.9 mEq. Next step is:

A. Vitamin D orally

B. Oral Ca2+ and vitamin D

C. Intravenous calcium gluconate and serial monitoring

D. Wait for Ca2+ to decrease to < 7.0 before taking further action

Ans. C

Q 222. A case of blunt trauma is brought to the emergency in a state of shock. He is not responding to IV crystalloids. Next step in his management would be:

A. Immediate laparotomy

B. Blood transfusion

C. Albumin transfusion

D. Abdominal compression

Ans. A

Q 223. A male is brought to the emergency as a case of road-traffic accident. He is hypotensive. Most likely ruptured organ is:

A. spleen

B. Mesentery

C. kidney

D. Rectum

Ans. A

Q 224. A patient is brought to the emergency as a case of head injury, following a head on collision road traffic accident. His BP is 90/60 mmHg. Tachycardia is present. Most likely diagnosis is:

A. EDH

B. SDH

C. Intracranial hemorrhage

D. Intra-abdominal bleed

Ans. D

Q 225. Ulcer that may develop in burn tissue is:

A. Marjolin

B. Rodent

C. Melanoma

D. Curling

Ans. A

Q 226. An elderly man presents with history of abdominal pain. He is found to have a fusiform dilatation of the descending aorta. Likely cause is:

A. Trauma

B. Atherosclerosis

C. Right ventricular failure

D. Syphilitic aortitis

Ans. B

Q 227. All of the following are correct regarding AV fistula except:

A. Arterialization of the veins

B. Proximal compression causes increase in heart rate

C. Overgrowth of a limb

D. Causes LV enlargement and LV failure

Ans. B

Q 228. All of the following are correct about axillary vein thrombosis except:

A. May be caused by a cervical rib

B. Treated with IV anticoagulant

C. Embolectomy is done in all cases

D. May occur following excessive exercise

Ans. C

Q 229. A 80 year old patient presents with a midline tumor of the lower jaw, involving the alveolar margin. He is edentulous. Treatment of choice is:

A. Hemimandibulectomy

B. Commando operation

C. Segmental mandiblectbmy

D. Marginal mandibulectomy

Ans. C

Q 230. Most common cause of unilateral parotid swelling in a 27 year old male is:

A. Warthin tumor

B. Pleomorphic adenoma

C. Adenocarcinoma

D. Haemangioma

Ans. B

Q 231. A 45 year old woman presents with a hard and mobile lump in the breast. Next investigation is:

A. FNAC

B. USG

C. Mammography

D. Excision biopsy

Ans. A

Q 232. A 45 years old man presents with progressive cervical lymph nodes enlargement since 3 month. Most diagnostic investigation is:

A. X-ray soft tissue

B. FNAC

C. Lymph node biopsy

D. None of the above

Ans. C

Q 233. All of the following are true about fibrolamellar carcinoma of the liver except:

A. Equal incidence in males and females

B. Better prognosis than HCC

C. AFP levels always greater than > 1000

D. Occur in younger individuals

Ans. C

Q 234. A child presents with an expansible swelling on medial side of the nose. Likely diagnosis is:

A. Teratoma

B. Meningocele

C. Dermoid cyst

D. Lipoma

Ans. B

Orthopaedics

Q 235. Following anterior dislocation of the shoulder, a patient develops weakness of flexion at elbow and lack of sensation over the lateral aspect fore arm. Nerve injured is:

A. Radial nerve

B. Musculocutaneous nerve

C. Axillary nerve

D. Ulnar nerve

Ans. B

Q 236. A 10 years old boy presents with FRACTURE of humerus. X-ray reveals a lytic lesion at the upper end. Likely condition is:

A. Unicameral bone cyst

B. Osteosarcoma

C. Osteoclastoma

D. Aneurysmal bone cyst

Ans. A

Q 237. A patient sustained injury to the upper limb 3 years back. He now presents with valgus deformity in the elbow and paresthesias over the medial border of the hand. The injury is likely to have been:

A. Supracondylar FRACTURE humerus

B. Lateral condyle FRACTURE humerus

C. Medial condyle FRACTURE humerus

D. Posterior dislocation of the humerus

Ans. B

Q 238. A woman aged 60 years suffers a fall. Her lower limb is abducted and externally rotated. Likely diagnosis is:

A. Neck of femur FRACTURE

B. Intertrochanteric femur FRACTURE

C. Posterior dislocation of hip

D. Anterior dislocation of hip

Ans. D

Q 239. Triple arthrodesis involves:

A. Calcaneocuboid, talonavicular and talocalcaneal

B. Tibiotalar, calcaneocuboid and talonavicular

C. Ankle joint, calcaneocuboid and talonavicular

D. None of the above

Ans. A

Q 240. Babu a 19 years old male has a small circumscribed sclerotic swelling over diaphysis of femur. Likely diagnosis is:

A. Osteoclastoma

B. Osteosarcoma

C. Ewing sarcoma

D. Osteoid osteoma

Ans. D

Q 241. Most common site of osteogenic sarcoma is:

A. Femur, upper end

B. Femur, lower end

C. Tibia, upper end

D. Tibia, lower end

Ans. B

Q 242. Involvement of PIP joint, DIP joint and the carpometacarpal joint of base of thumb with sparing the wrist is seen in:

A. Rheumatoid arthritis

B. Osteoarthritis

C. Psoriatic arthritis

D. Pseudogout

Ans. B

Q 243. The pivot test is for:

A. Anterior cruciate ligament

B. Posterior cruciate ligament

C. Medial meniscus

D. Lateral meniscus

Ans. A

Q 244. Iliotibial band contracture following polio is likely to result in:

A. Extension at hip

B. Extension at knee

C. Flexion at hip and knee

D. Extension at hip and knee

Ans. C

Anaesthesia

Q 245. All of the following agents can be given for induction of Anaesthesia in children except:

A. Halothane

B. Servoflurane

C. Morphine

D. Nitrous oxide

Ans. C

Q 246. Anaesthetic agent of choice in renal failure is:

A. Methoxyflurane

B. Isoflurane

C. Enflurane

D. None of the above

Ans. B

Q 247. A man with alcoholic liver failure requires general Anaesthesia for Surgery . Anaesthetic agent of choice is:

A. Ether

B. Halothane

C. Methoxyflurane

D. Isoflurane

Ans. D

Q 248. All of the following are true except:

A. Halothane is good as an analgesic agent

B. Halothane sensitises the heart to action of catacholamines

C. Halothane relaxes brochi & is preferred as anaesthetics

D. Halothane may cause liver cell necrosis

Ans. A

Ophthalmology

Q 249. A patient has a miotic pupil, IOP= 25, normal anterior chamber, hazy cornea and a shallow anterior chamber in fellow eye. Diagnosis is:

A. Acute anterior uveitis

B. Acute angle closure glaucoma

C. Acute open angle glaucoma

D. Senile cataract

Ans. A

Q 250. A woman complains of coloured haloes around lights in the evening, with nausea and vomiting, IOP is normal. Diagnosis is:

A. Incipient stage, glaucoma open angle

B. Prodromal stage, closed angle glaucoma

C. Migraine

D. Raised ICT

Ans. B

Q 251. Babloo, a 5 years old child, presents with large cornea, lacrimation and photophobia. Diagnosis is:

A. Megalocornea

B. Congenital glaucoma

C. Congenital cataract

D. Anterior uveitis

Ans. B

Q 252. Herpes zoster ophthalmicus causes all except:

A. Nummular keratitis

B. Vitreal haemorrhage

C. Uveitis

D. Cranial nerve palsies

Ans. B

Q 253. Bilateral ptosis is not seen in:

A. Marfan syndrome

B. Myaesthenia gravis

C. Myotonic dystrophy

D. Kearns-Sayre syndrome

Ans. A

Q 254. eye is deviated laterally and downwards and patient is unable to look up or medially. Likely nerve involved is:

A. Trochlear

B. Trigeminal

C. Oculomotor

D. Abducent

Ans. C

Q 255. Left sided lateral gaze is affected in lesion of:

A. Right frontal lobe

B. Right occipital lobe

C. Left occipital lobe

D. Left frontal lobe

Ans. A

Q 256. An elderly male with heart disease presents with sudden loss of vision in one eye. Examination reveals cherry red spot. Diagnosis is:

A. Central retinal vein occlusion

B. Central retinal artery occlusion

C. Amaurosis fugax

D. Acute ischemic optic neuritis

Ans. B

Q 257. Which of following is not a feature in diabetic retinopathy on fundus examination?

A. Microaneurysms

B. Retinal hemorrhages

C. Arteriolar dilatation

D. Neovascularisation

Ans. C

Q 258. Vitamin B12 deficiency is likely to cause:

A. Bitemporal hemianopia

B. Binasal hemianopia

C. Heteronymous hemianopia

D. Centrocecal scotoma

Ans. D

Q 259. All are true regarding optic neuritis except:

A. Decreased visual acuity

B. Decreased pupillary reflex

C. Abnormal electroretinogram

D. Abnormal visual evoked response retinogram

Ans. C

Q 260. Chalky white optic disc on fundus examination is seen in all except:

A. Syphilis

B. Leber hereditary optic neuropathy

C. Post papilledema optic neuritis

D. Traumatic injury to the optic nerve

Ans. D

ENT

Q 261. A 3 months old child presents with intermittent stridor. Most likely cause is:

A. Laryngotracheobronchitis

B. Laryngomalacia

C. Respiratory obstruction

D. Foreign body aspiration

Ans. B

Q 262. A patient presents with facial nerve palsy following head trauma with FRACTURE of the mastoid. Best intervention here is:

A. Immediate decompression

B. Wait and watch

C. Facial sling

D. Steroids

Ans. A

Q 263. A case of Bell palsy on steroids shows no improvement after 2 weeks. The next step in management should be:

A. Vasodilators and ACTH

B. Physiotherapy and electrical stimulation

C. Increase steroid dosage

D. Electrophysiological nerve testing

Ans. D

Q 264. Chandu a 15 years aged boy presents with unilateral nasal blockade, mass in the cheek and epistaxis. Likely diagnosis is:

A. Nasopharyngeal CA

B. Angiofibroma

C. Inverted papilloma

D. None of the above

Ans. B

Q 265. A 40 years old diabetic presents with blackish nasal discharge and a mass in the nose . Likely diagnosis is:

A. Mucormycosis

B. Actinomycosis

C. Rhinosporiodosis

D. Histoplasmosis

Ans. A

Q 266. Most radiosensitive tumour of the following is:

A. Supraglortic CA

B. CA glottis

C. CA nasopharynx

D. Subglottic CA

Ans. C

OBSTETRICS & Gynaecology

Q 267. Rokitansky Kuster Hauser syndrome is associated with:

A. Ovarian agenesis

B. Absent fallopian tube

C. Vaginal atresia

D. Bicornuate uterus

Ans. C

Q 268. A patient of 47 XXY karyotype presents with features of hypogonadism. The likely diagnosis is:

A. Turner syndrome

B. Klinefelter syndrome

C. Edward syndrome

D. Down syndrome

Ans. B

Q 269. A girl presents with primary amenorrhea, grade V thelarche, grade II pubarche, no axillary hair. The likely diagnosis is:

A. Testicular feminization

B. Mullerian agenesis

C. Turner syndrome

D. Gonadal dysgenesis

Ans. A

Q 270. A woman presents with amenorrhea of 6 weeks duration and lump in the right iliac fossa. Investigation of choice is:

A. USG abdomen

B. Laparoscopy

C. CT scan

D. Shielded X-ray

Ans. A

Q 271. A woman presents with amenorrhea of 2 months duration lower abdominal pain, facial pallor, fainting and shock. Diagnosis is:

A. Ruptured ovarian cyst

B. Ruptured ecotopic pregnancy

C. Threatened abortion

D. Septic abortion

Ans. B

Q 272. A young woman with six weeks amenorrhea presents with mass abdomen. USG shows empty uterus. Diagnosis is:

A. Ovarian cyst

B. Ectopic pregnancy

C. Complete abortion

D. None of the above

Ans. B

Q 273. A 30 years old female, presents to the emergency with complaint of sudden severe abdominal pain. An abdominal mass is palpable on examination. Most likely diagnosis is:

A. Torsion of subserous fibroid

B. Torsion of ovarian cyst

C. Rupture of ectopic pregnancy

D. Rupture of ovarian cyst

Ans. B

Q 274. A 28 years aged female with a history of 6 weeks of amenorrhea, presents with pain in abdomen. USG shows fluid in pouch of Douglas. Aspiration yields dark colour blood that fails to clot. Most probable diagnosis is:

A. Ruptured ovarian cyst

B. Ruptured ectopic pregnancy

C. Red degeneration of fibroid

D. Pelvic abscess

Ans. B

Q 275. A patient complains of post coital bleed. No growth is seen on per speculum examination. Next step should be:

A. Colposcopic biopsy

B. Conization

C. Pap smear

D. Culdoscopy

Ans. A

Q 276. A 50 years old woman presents with post coital bleeding. A visible growth on cervix is detected on per speculum examination. Next investigation is:

A. Punch biopsy

B. Colposcopic biopsy

C. Pap smear

D. Cone biopsy

Ans. A

Q 277. A 45 years woman, has negative pap smear with +ve endocervical curretage. Next step in management will be:

A. Colposcopy

B. Vaginal hysterectomy

C. Conization

D. Wartheim hysterectomy

Ans. D

Q 278. A case of carcinoma cervix is found in altered sensorium and is having hiccups. The likely cause is:

A. Septicemia

B. Uremia

C. Raised ICT

D. Intestinal obstruction

Ans. B

Q 279. Bilateral ovarian cancer with capsule breached, ascites positive for malignant cells. Stage is:

A. I

B. II

C. III

D. IV

Ans. B

Q 280. The true regarding adenomyosis is:

A. More common in nullipara

B. Progestins are the agents of choice for medical management

C. Presents with menorrhagia, dysmenorrhoea, and an enlarged uterus

D. More common in young women

Ans. C

Q 281. In an infertile woman, endometrial biopsy reveals proliferative changes. Which hormone should be preferred?

A. MDPA

B. Desogestrel

C. Norethisterone

D. None of the above

Ans. A

Q 282. A patient semen sample reveals: 15 million sperms/ml, 60 % normal morphology, 60% motile sperms volume is 2 ml; no agglutination is seen. Diagnosis is:

A. Azoospermia

B. Aspermia

C. Oligospermia

D. Normospermia

Ans. C

Q 283. Primary peritonitis is more common in females because:

A. Ostia of fallopian tubes communicate with abdominal cavity

B. Peritoneum overlies the uterus

C. Rupture of functional ovarian cysts

D. None of the above.

Ans. A

Q 284. False statement regarding HCG is:

A. It is secreted by cytotrophoblasts

B. It acts on same receptor as LH does

C. It has luteotrophic action

D. It is a glycoprotein

Ans. A

Q 285. All of the following are false except:

A. Oxytocin sensitivity increased during delivery

B. Prostaglandins should be given during 2nd trimester

C. Ergot derivatives relax lower segment of uterus

D. Oxytocin is best for induction of labour in IUD

Ans. A

Q 286. Snow storm appearance on USG is seen in:

A. Hydatidiform mole

B. Ectopic pregnancy

C. Anencephaly

D. None of the above

Ans. A

Q 287. All of the following are indications for termination of pregnancy in APH patient except:

A. 37 weeks

B. IUD

C. Transverse lie

D. Continous bleeding

Ans. C

Q 288. A lady with 37 weeks pregnancy, presented with bleeding per vagina. Invetigation shows severe degree of placenta previa. The treatment is:

A. Immediate CS

B. Blood transfusion

C. Conservative

D. Medical induction of labour

Ans. A

Q 289. A pregnant woman presents with red degeneration of fibroid. Management is:

A. Myomectomy

B. Conservative

C. Hysterectomy

D. Termination of pregnancy

Ans. B

Q 290. An ovarian cyst is detected in a pregnant woman. Management is:

A. Immediate removal by laprotomy

B. Wait and watch

C. Removal by laparotomy in second trimester

D. Remove at time of caesarean section

Ans. C

Q 291. Most useful investigation in the first trimester to identify risk of fetal malformation in a fetus of a diabetic mother is:

A. Glycosylated Hb

B. Ultrasound

C. MS-AFP

D. Amniocentesis

Ans. A

Q 292. A pregnant diabetic on oral sulphonyl urea therapy is shifted to insulin. All of the followings are true regarding this, except:

A. Oral hypoglycaemics cause PIH

B. Insulin does not cross placenta

C. Oral hypoglycaemics cross placenta and deplete fetal insulin

D. During pregnancy insulin requirement increases and cannot be met with sulphonylureas

Ans. A

Q 293. Condition associated with lack of a

A. Robert pelvis

B. Naegele pelvis

C. Rachitic pelvis

D. Osteomalacia pelvis

Ans. B

Q 294. Consequence of maternal use of cocaine is:

A. Hydrops fetalis

B. Sacral agenesis

C. Cerebral infarction

D. Hypertrichosis

Ans. C

Q 295. DNA analysis of chorionic villus/amniocentesis is not likely to detect:

A. Tay Sachs disease

B. Hemophilia A

C. Sickle cell disease

D. Duchenne muscular dystrophy

Ans. A

Q 296. A woman has had 2 previous anencephalic babies, risk of having a third one is:

A. 0%

B. 10%

C. 25%

D. 50%

Ans. B

Radiology

Q 297. A neonate presents with respiratory distress, contralateral mediastinal shift and multiple cystic airfilled lesions in the chest. Most likely diagnosis is:

A. Congenital diaphragmatic hernia

B. Congenital lung cysts

C. Pneumonia

D. None of the above

Ans. A

Q 298. Ground glass appearance is not seen in:

A. Hyaline membrane disease

B. Pneumonia

C. Left to right shunt

D. Obstructive TAPVC

Ans. C

Q 299. Drug that is radioprotective:

A. Paclitaxel

B. Vincristine

C. Amifostine

D. Etoposide

Ans. C

Q 300. Most radiosensitive tumour of the following is:

A. CA kidney

B. CA colon

C. CA pancreas

D. CA cervix

Ans. D

ALL THE BEST FOR YOUR EXAMS

Printed by Libri Plureos GmbH in Hamburg,
Germany